CHRIST
AND
HISTORY

CHRIST
AND
HISTORY

George Arthur Buttrick

ABINGDON PRESS

NEW YORK   NASHVILLE

CHRIST AND HISTORY

Copyright © 1963 by Abingdon Press

Library of Congress Catalog Card Number: 63-11376

"God's World," Edna St. Vincent Millay, copyright 1913-1940 by Edna St. Vincent Millay.

"Recessional" and "The Prayer of Miriam Cohen," Rudyard Kipling, reprinted by permission of Mrs. George Bambridge and Doubleday & Co., Inc.

"The Everlasting Mercy" and "The Widow in the Bye Street," John Masefield, by permission of The Macmillan Co.

"Let Us Honor if We Can" from Poems, by W. H. Auden. Copyright 1934 and renewed 1961 by W. H. Auden. Reprinted by permission of Random House, Inc., and Faber and Faber Ltd.

"For the Time Being," by W. H. Auden. Copyright 1944 by W. H. Auden. Reprinted from The Collected Poetry of W. H. Auden, by permission of Random House, Inc., and Faber and Faber Ltd.

Scripture quotations unless otherwise noted are from the Revised Standard Version of the Bible, copyrighted 1946 and 1952 by the Division of Christian Education, National Council of Churches, and are used by permission.

SET UP, PRINTED, AND BOUND BY THE PARTHENON PRESS, AT NASHVILLE, TENNESSEE, UNITED STATES OF AMERICA

FOR
ANN, HILARY and MICHAEL

Χάρις ὑμῖν καὶ εἰρήνη ἀπὸ
θεοῦ πατρὸς ἡμῶν καὶ
κυρίου Ἰησοῦ Χριστοῦ

PREFACE

A PREFACE USUALLY OFFERS "REASONS" WHY THE AUTHOR HAS written the book, and is sometimes half-apology. The occasion which prompted this book is told in the Prologue, and also the conviction which the book offers. But the "reasons" for my writing the book are one reason: I "had" to write it. The material in these pages grew from lectures delivered under several lectureships. But I did not accept these generous invitations simply because they came, and because I must therefore "find a suitable topic." No, there was a word I must speak. I had been dismayed by our unthinking acceptance of Arnold Toynbee's *A Study of History* on the one hand and, on the other hand, by our glib trust in American "progress." The Bible, the deep wisdom of which persists and may one day prevail, denies that we are trapped either in a circular prison or on an ascending escalator. More and more I said to myself and others: "Oh, that men knew the fatefulness, the zest, the cruciality, and the once-for-all-encounter of the Biblical truth concerning history!" Therefore this book. Other projected books were on my desk in rough draft or fuller writing. One was in completed manuscript awaiting further light. But they were pushed aside: I had to write this book.

As for the lectureships, four of these chapters were presented as the Auburn Lectures in Union Theological Seminary, New York City in the fall of 1960. President Henry P. Van Dusen and Professor Frank O. Reed were my kind advisors. The same four chapters, with but one change, were given as the Rall Lectures in Garrett Theological Seminary in Evanston, Illinois in the spring of 1961; there President Dwight E. Loder and Dean John C. Irwin were generous and rash enough to be my sponsors. Six chapters in lecture form comprised the William Belden Noble Lectures at Harvard University in the fall of 1962;

7

there President Nathan M. Pusey and the Reverend R. Jerrold Gibson, acting minister in Memorial Church, risked some dark fate by their outright encouragement. One chapter was given as a lecture in Baldwin Wallace College, and another was read to the Faculty of Colgate-Rochester Seminary. In each place discussions with faculty and students corrected and clarified my mind, but did not dissuade me from the central faith. Gratitude to all these friends goes far beyond my best words.

Thanks are offered also to Miss Marilyn Butt who typed the manuscript at short notice and in brief time span, yet with care and skill. My wife, Agnes Gardner Buttrick, has compiled the notes and the indices. No one could have been more thorough and patient in research. My memory is voluminous, but not always accurate. So this book could hardly have been prepared or printed without her help. Indeed all my work has rested on her loyalty. My sons also lent their aid, perhaps especially David with some incisive comments on the chapter on "The Paradox of History." Again the gratitude is deep: this printed acknowledgement is hardly more than hint.

As I write, the Cuban crisis darkens over us. How can any action in history avoid blindness unless we know the meaning of history? I am sure that the truth in these pages is pertinent, maybe as pertinent as a surgeon's scalpel set against a festering wound. Is it conceit to believe that the Biblical verity about history has not elsewhere been so pointedly stated, or so forthrightly applied to the cruciality of present history? Perhaps it is: so I ask God's forgiveness. But perhaps it is not, for these pages are not mainly mine: they came as gift upon partial blindness. So with penitence for blindness and too great confidence, and with gratitude for granted grace, this book is sent on its way. May He bless it, with furtherance or denial, Who came among us "in great humility."

GEORGE A. BUTTRICK
Wilmette, Illinois
October 1962

CONTENTS

Prologue 11

1. The Bible and History 15

2. The Focus of History 30

3. History and Progress 45

4. History as Paradox 63

5. History, Necessity,
   and Freedom 82

6. History as Revelation 99

7. History and Tragedy 119

8. The Fulfillment of History   138

Notes   159

Index of Scripture   169

Index of Persons
    and Subjects   171

Prologue

THIS LITTLE BOOK "BEGAN" ON A CERTAIN NIGHT IN HARVARD University after a lecture by Arnold Toynbee. He was facile, articulate, charming, plausible, persuasive, immensely erudite— and mistaken. My students listened in crowded Sanders Theater with glowing faces. I overtook one of them after the lecture on his way back to The Yard, and this was the conversation between learner-teacher and learner-student:

Teacher: "You didn't swallow all of it?"
Student: "Wasn't it wonderful?"
Teacher: "Not very."
Student: "What was wrong with it?"
Teacher: "If history is cyclic, then, even though the cycles are as enormous as civilizations, history is a squirrel-cage. How do you like being one of the squirrels?"
Student: "But he said that our civilization can break through the circle."
Teacher: "Yes, but since all the others have gone an intricate charted pathway to the laundry or the cemetery, why should ours survive?"
Student: "But you don't believe in some chamber-of-commerce doctrine of guaranteed progress?"
Teacher: "No, for that also would kill any real freedom; we would be dummies riding an escalator."
Student: "Then what do you believe?"
Teacher: "You think it through. One of our course books has both appreciation and criticism for Mr. Toynbee."
Student: "Which book?"

11

Teacher: "You are supposed to be reading it. When you find it come over to our home, if you are so minded, and we can talk about it."

The book in question was Reinhold Niebuhr's *Faith and History*. That student came, and we had some hours of give-and-take, not in debate which settles nothing, but in a sharing of minds. Then there was the following:

Student: "Why don't you throw out four or five of your lectures, and write about history?"

Teacher: " 'Throw out' is the right word. They should all be thrown out. But I would like to sometime."

The "sometime" did not come at Harvard. My work there multiplied in college and seminary and church, with pastoral demands and endless counseling added to the burden. Soon it was too heavy; wisely and rightly I yielded the task to younger shoulders. But in somewhat easier emeritus years I began to read in the theory of history.

Then came the invitation to deliver The William Belden Noble Lectures at Harvard. Year by year it had been an item of my duty to suggest to President Pusey the name of the Noble lecturer. How generous of him and others to invite me to return from emeritus semi-purgatory! It was characteristic sequel to the characteristic friendship which, amid spells of turbulence, was generously shown me for six years in the precincts of Harvard Square, which is crossed by only two species of human creatures, "the quick and the dead." The summons intensified the reading in historical theory, for nobody may lecture at Harvard who has not "done the reading," even though the reading may be to little purpose except as mortification of the flesh. Much of my reading was not nectar, but it has been swallowed—like medicine. This book hardly hints the labor.

Thus came these chapters on the biblical view of history. The view may be accepted or refused, but it is not tedious. It is as exciting as radium. This doctrine is no cage for squirrels or moving staircase for robots. It sees history as a Dialogue between God and man-on-pilgrimage in the language of events. There are recurrences in the Conversation (Toynbee's cycles) as in any dialogue, and newnesses (American "progress") as in any dialogue. There are unresolved mysteries, for God begins, continues, and ends the interchange. There is many a bafflement, for His thoughts are not our thoughts. But sometimes there is a breakthrough of light. Is Christ the key to the translation? Sometimes the man says "no" to God, and God waits while life darkens; and sometimes the man says "yes," and God waits while life gathers in joy. Is prayer the quiet booth where the Conversation can best be heard and understood?

In any event this doctrine of history has fatefulness and daily surprise. The man in the Dialogue opens his newspaper each morning, checks off the events, and asks, "What does the Silence mean in this happening?" The biblical view of history gives life dimension (what dimension!), fatefulness, encounter, rapture and darkness, Judgment and Mercy—and the persuasion that history shall be fulfilled beyond the gates of time.

CHAPTER I

The Bible and History

IN OUR BROKEN TIME WE REALIZE THAT HISTORY HAS A SPHINXLIKE face, but our secular wisdom does not turn to the Bible for answer to the riddle. The Bible is "old stuff." The skepticism which began in the Renaissance and became explicit in Hume[1] damaged Bible reading. The Book itself set barriers even in its physical form, for it was usually bound in black, with print that taxed the eyes, and set in double columns with margins providing dubious references. The newer knowledge raised still higher blocks. We learned, for instance, about undeniable links between the religion of Israel and the other faiths of the Fertile Crescent, and we had no mind to trace the sharp differences; and, as darker disfigurement, there were contradictions both in fact and in ethic within the Bible itself. So the heady wine of the new knowledge had little use for what men deemed the stale water of the Scriptures. Some people still read the Book, they being the seed of the Church. Others read it not at all, or only in crisis, hoping it might prove a magic raft in the storm.

But now man's wisdom has led to an impasse. His trust in native intelligence and good will is confounded. Perhaps the Bible has a solving word, perhaps the solving word: here and there such is the pondering of our time. The trouble is that the Bible, especially to men who have passed it by, does not always offer its gold in nuggets. It is a mountain range whose wealth must be mined, smelted, and refined. Will people fed on magazine literature pay that price? If so, they might find in the Bible a tremendous doctrine of time, which makes our clock theories seem a kindergarten fancy; a doctrine of man so daring in its

15

paradox that by comparison American optimism and existential despair alike appear half-baked; a doctrine of God so far from "pious" that it has the surge and mystery of an ocean; and a doctrine of history, this being our present concern, which historians only now begin to explore. Other books ply the safe waters of Long Island Sound: this Book goes "down to the sea," to do "business on the great waters." [2] So we ask as introductory question, "What of the Bible and History?"

I

The initial answer is that the Bible is history, though it should be specially noted, *it is history after its own kind*. It tells the story of one people, a Bedouin tribe at the first, set in the midst of all people. It recounts the life of men, their bonds with field and sky; their politics, as when Assyria "came down like the wolf on the fold," [3] or Pilate delivered Christ to be crucified; their economics: should the poor be sold for a pair of shoes,[4] or the early Christians pay Caesar's taxes?;[5] their friendships and hates, their sexual passions and their fears, their homes and daily work, their life and the bleak oncoming of death. Wealthy men bid preachers "stick to the Bible." They little know, these critics (or even some of the preachers), that the Bible sticks to them at every step of their pilgrimage. It is an instant and earthy Book.

Rudolf Bultmann has left us in debt. He has almost given New Testament study a bold, new turn. But certain demurrers are in order. The main trouble is not with his undue concern to mollify the scientific mind, though it is undue at a time when our age is more and more suspicious of science as a savior; nor is it in his failure (though there is partial failure) to distinguish between myth and symbol and between nature-myth and history-myth; nor is it with his choice of Heidegger's existentialism as the new idiom for the Gospels, though that ontology is too rarified for one man in a hundred to understand. No, the main trouble is in his thesis that the New Testament is basically myth.[6] There is obviously interpretation in the Gospels. They

16

are indeed a faith-proclamation, necessarily written in the language and thought-forms of their time; and they involve mythic elements. But their core is history, not myth. Even the great creeds turn back into the history from which they came: "Jesus Christ . . . suffered under Pontius Pilate, was crucified, dead, and buried. . . . The third day he rose again from the dead." [7] The Bible at base is history.

Furthermore Bible history claims to be the binding thread of all history in the sense that its events are the revelatory light which gives meaning to the whole panorama of man's story. Arnold Toynbee alleges that "the Jews suffered from the illusion that they were "not a but the 'chosen people.'" [8] He thus includes the biblical claim with a whole series of drab national egotisms. But he is not always perceptive and not always well-informed. There is a profound difference between the Old Testament claim, on the one hand, and Hitler's "Blood and Soil" [9] or even our "American Dream" on the other hand. For Israel at best knew that the choice involved no merit in the chosen, but only the mystery of God's inscrutable will. [10] The choice, moreover, was not for favor so that Israel might bask in God's exclusive sunlight, but for commission so that through Israel "all the nations of the earth [might] be blessed." [11] Furthermore, Israel knew that in her disobedience the choice would become God's stern judgment: "a day of darkness, and not light." [12] There was a still deeper understanding: Israel came to see that her very suffering might be fulfillment of her mission, as the "Suffering Servant" passages of Deutero-Isaiah poignantly testify. [13] As last item of difference, Israel looked beyond her present history to a new messianic outpouring of God's grace. We may rightly ask what likeness can here be found to national and tribal egocentricities.

So the Bible is history. This historicity in the warp and woof of Scripture is unimpressed by our intellectual fashions. We ask for an ideology, little realizing that only insensate pride would presume to write a prescription for all men for all time; but the Bible replies, "Do you remember what happened to Pharaoh?"

We demand "proof" of God, forgetting that if we could prove
God He would be within the compass of our rationalities, and
that then our logical mind would be our own grotesque God;
but the Bible answers, "Once a Man was being crucified, and
God seemed to have deserted him, but he died still commend-
ing himself to God." We require a theology, or, better, an intellectual philosophy, for a philosophy is more fashionable than
a theology; but the Bible asks, "Have you heard about Micaiah,[14]
or about Demas who 'loved this present world'?" [15] The Bible
is not a philosophy of God's Being: it is a history of men under
God's acts of visitation and constraint. This historicity is exasperating, especially to an academic community. It offers no
comfort to an ivory tower. Nay, it raises questions about the
nature of mind. Is thought primarily scientific or philosophical
or theological? Or is it historical, that is, so constituted as to be
able by nature to respond to the onsets of God in history? At
any rate, the Bible *is* history.

II

Next: the Bible is history under God. It is sacred history, the
account of God's dealings with one people who, despite history's
always distinctive thrust, are in some sense microcosm of all
people. We speak of "man's quest for God." The Bible so
speaks, but only because it first speaks of God's quest for man.
For the Bible never forgets that man is the creature, and that
God in whatever mystery is God the Creator. The Bible does
not argue "the existence of God." That very phrase makes God
a mere "existent." No, the Bible says that we live under "the
stigma of finitude," [16] and thus dimly know the Unconditioned;
and that Mystery is always breaking in on our human pilgrimage.
Yes, the God of the Bible dwells in heaven above our time and
space, and above our spectrum of right and wrong; but the Bible
mainly portrays Him as Creator of men and Lord of history.
His Name or nature is revealed in "His mighty acts." Thus for
the Old Testament the focus of His revelation, the event which
casts light on all events, is the sequence of "wonders" which He

18

wrought for Israel—the triumph over Pharaoh, the crossing of the Sea of Reeds, and the settlement in the Promised Land. For the New Testament these "acts of God" are the still more wondrous events of Galilee, Calvary, and Easter Day.

The Bible does not bar our theologies: it provides material for them. But its major concern is not with our theological understanding, but with our willed response to God's onsets. It says, "Yes, your pondering of the mystery of suffering will bring you to antinomies, the postulation of great thunders in the Abyss —God as Victim, God as Victor; God as wrath, God as love; God as Being, God as Non-Being. But your mind cannot resolve an antinomy. Meanwhile you have a life to live in history. Where does light break on you, since truth is the breakthrough of light? Walk in the light by the power of the light, in faith!" An exasperating Book! Perhaps the right translation of the Divine Name, "I AM THAT I AM," [17] is, as some modern scholars have proposed, some such phrase as, "I WILL TO DO WHAT I WILL TO DO." [18] That version is certainly true to the Bible's existential stance. In a not-forbidden way of pondering, the Bible is closer to economics and politics than to theology.

So, to the Bible, our history, social and personal, is an awestruck affair, a Divine encounter. "The earth is the Lord's and the fulness thereof, the world and those who dwell therein." [19] Our politics are not merely messy, nor our economics merely contentious: no, a "shadowy third" [20] is always interrupting these dialogues between man and man. There are blights and seductions on nature and human nature which we do not understand (Luther called them, "God's alien work"),[21] and outright disobediences and blasphemies which we understand all too well. But God made our world and life (Luther again: "God's proper work"),[22] and looked on it, and saw "that it was good." [23] So, to the Bible, our life is not humdrum. It is our reply day by day to God's onsets in history in the light of his focal onset in Christ. Our work and play thus become a vitality and a deeper wonder. The repeated song in a modern musical play is essentially biblical: "A hundred thousand miracles are happening

19

every day." [24] This planet is not unworthy, but rather the scene of a strange conversation between God and men; not, as Greek thought would hold, a prison for the soul or the work of an evil demi-urge, as though God had a half-wit brother in charge of concretion while He Himself dwelt in some remote Tranquility, but the place of God's visitation. That is why the Bible is a book of history, and why the Bible sees our world and life as Encounter shot through with surprise and darkness, with grief and great laughter.

III

The Bible is therefore from our human side faith history, the story of man's response to God's acts. All history is, of course, faith history. Secular history, with no room for any belief in God, is nevertheless faith history: it assumes that life is merely secular, a poor creature of time and space, and the assumption may be very surprised ten seconds after death. Likewise objective history is faith history: it is written in the pretense that there is no subject, or that the subject has eyes as neutral as a camera. We live in a strange time, when science tries to liquidate the subject, and some existentialism tries to liquidate the object. So the Bible is faith-history. It says, because it is honest with life, "We are gripped by Mystery, in birth and in death, in disaster and sudden tenderness"; and it responds to the Mystery in worship and daily life. Such is the very nature of faith. There is therefore always an ultimate reference in Bible history. Assyria's invasion could be described in terms of politics and economics, of course, but that description, by Biblical conviction, is short-circuited, for God's purposes were afoot in the national crisis. Maybe communism is the scourge of the Lord; maybe our pride and comfort are a breach of the covenant. At any rate such surmises are after the manner of Biblical faith. It is certain that history does not fulfill human plans and hopes. There is Mystery and faith's reply. History is a Dialogue between God and man in the language of events.

Faith history in its recording is not pedant about literal fact.

Contradictions in population figures or in war-casualties in the Bible story should neither surprise nor dismay us. Men are never infallible or free from regional pride. The main concern is meaning, not facticity. Do not misunderstand: the Bible story has both actuality and accuracy, as archeology remarkably attests in our time. But there is no worship of literalness, just as there are no perfect scribes. The statistics in The Book of Chronicles are in rounded and almost stylized numbers, which do not agree with the figures given in The Book of Kings; but there is more honesty in being right as to meanings (in this instance the obligation to keep the Covenant) and wrong on numbers than there is in our modern mind which is scientifically careful about statistics and does not even ask about meanings.

At any rate the Bible records man's response to the onsets of the Mystery. It tells not only

> Of man's first disobedience, and the fruit
> Of that forbidden tree, whose mortal taste
> Brought death into the world, and all our woe [25]

but of our continued rebellion and return. Thus the ethical inconsistencies of Scripture. This is faith-history, the account of man's response to God's search: our dim or bright understanding, our denial or consent. Why should we ask ethical consistency? There are no human angels. When was any man free of local prejudice? When were we completely purged of self-interest? So there are bloodthirsty pages in the Bible. What would we expect in a book of faith-history: a prim Samuel Smiles [26] or a moralistic Mrs. Grundy? [27] The Bible shows a man who now is "after God's own heart," [28] but soon is deliberately planning and practicing adultery.[29] No honest writer of history, especially of faith-history, can prettify the human scene. Oliver Cromwell instructed the artist to whom he was sitting for a portrait to depict him "with all my warts." [30] Why should we ask anything else of the Bible? But it never shows man as walking alone: he is always under the thunders and daybreaks of the Mystery.

Such history will naturally include far more than a dull hatchment of "facts," supposing there were such things as "bare facts." All facts come clothed with interpretation, if only with the thought forms of their time; and all facts are reclothed by this and that later historian. The Bible admits the inevitable stance, and boldly asks which stance is true. So the Bible includes great myths, such as Babel and Armageddon. Why not? People in history cannot help asking about the Mystery in which history begins and ends, and therefore all rightful telling of the human story should incorporate myths, which are the adumbration of total history. The Bible includes stories also, lovely stories such as that of

> ... the sad heart of Ruth, when, sick for home,
> She stood in tears amid the alien corn;[31]

and harshly nationalistic stories such as that of Esther. The Bible has poems also, of existential despair (the original Job is perhaps the Franz Kafka of the Old Testament), and of courage ("The Lord is my light and my salvation; whom shall I fear?"),[32] and of quiet trust ("The Lord is my shepherd").[33] But surely history is poor history that finds no place for a people's songs and prayers. The Bible has sermons also, by false prophets and true prophets, the former telling of " 'Peace, peace,' when there is no peace"; [34] and the latter proclaiming the midnight of God's judgments and the new dawn of His mercy. Why not? Sermons should both pierce and heal their time. So the Bible is history, and sacred history, and faith-history.

IV

Now a double word: the Bible tells both of history's brokenness and history's redemption. As to the brokenness, the Bible is blunt: history has a fatal flaw. Compare this honesty with the Marxist dialectic ending in a stainless steel paradise. Compare it with Hegelian optimism supposed to come to climax in the perfect Prussian state. Compare it with American faith in the natural goodness of man and the endlessness of material progress. Then be grateful for the honesty of the Bible story. The man in the street is on the side of the Bible. He has deeper insight than philosophers: he knows that "there is something wrong with the world." Bible pages are bloody—because men are violent. Bible pages tell of patriarchs visiting prostitutes—for human story has never been free of that stigma. There is no Pollyanna in Scripture, and for that we may be thankful: she is a revoltingly sugary child. Think of her with her cargo of molasses at Buchenwald! [35] The Bible says that the world of nature, which is the stage of history (and more than stage because our bodies are part of nature) is flawed or groaning in travail; and it says even more insistently that human nature is flawed: "None is righteous, no, not one." [36] The Bible never surveys our human story with amoral or merely objective eyes, for there is no such view. It confronts the fact that there is cancer in nature (is there not?), and egocentricity both subtle and violent in human nature. To this theme modern literature now returns, as in Albert Camus' *The Fall*,[37] or Robert Penn Warren's *Brother to Dragons*.[38]

But whereas our modern mind now despairs, Bible history speaks in one breath of history's brokenness and history's promise. Man in the Bible is always on tiptoe, straining his eyes for the first light of dawn. We are so accustomed to this hope that we miss its startling newness. Compare Buddhist history, which is not history: illusion rather, the stain of existence, from which a man must seek present escape in contemplation and final escape in Nirvana. Compare Hindu history, child of Greek cyclicism, with its endless round of reincarnations, oblivion being the only escape from the wheel. There is not much purpose in Arnold Toynbee's glib bracketing of "the four great religions," except to a shallow and unexamined syncretism.[39] I tell my granddaughter a story: "'Twas a wild and stormy night: the wind moaned in the rigging, the waves washed high over the decks, the stars were blotted out in blackness; and the captain in the cabin told the first mate this story: 'Twas a wild and stormy night.'" After the second time around Anne says, "That's silly!" After the fourth

23

time, she says, "I don't want to hear anymore." Anne is a historian—in the great Biblical tradition. For there is movement in Biblical history, though it is not to be confused with our fuzzy ideas of progress,[40] still less with ideas of inevitable evolution: Bible history is life-drama with plot and pilgrimage and dénouement. Such history is a new thing under the sun, part of the striking uniqueness of Scripture.

Bible history is the outworking of God's mysterious purpose always partly hidden, always partly understood. Thus Abraham leaves the carnal itch of Ur to seek a city "which has foundations." [41] In that search he makes a nation, which falls into captivity. In captivity they foresee a promised land, and find it through the deliverance at the Sea of Reeds. Again they are made captive, to surmise, in the heartbreaking insight of Second Isaiah, that their very suffering may become the seed of a new Israel. When that insight is unfulfilled, the apocalyptists insist in lurid imagery that a Messenger shall come to shatter "this sorry Scheme of Things" [42] with all its wickedness, to reward the saints, and to establish "a new heaven and a new earth." [43] Then Jesus. Bible history is eschatalogical. It is a thrust into the unknown under the Divine will and purpose. It looks to the time beyond time when "loud voices in heaven" shall cry: "The kingdom of the world has become the kingdom of our Lord and of his Christ, and he shall reign forever and ever." [44]

Do we laugh at such a dream as a "thing incredible"? This "forwardness" in Biblical history, contra any view of history as static or cyclic, has so set the fashion of our modern mind (for there were times when men were steeped in the Bible) that we first take it for granted and then distort it. We take it for granted: every scientist believes there is more to be learned about nature (science is not a squirrel cage), and every politician promises a better world, though neither scientist nor politician is quick to confess his debt to the Bible. Then, having adopted the Biblical hope, we distort it. Under the influence of biological science we equate it with a fancied "evolution" in human society. Under the influence of technological advance we deem it a guarantee

24

of "progress" towards human perfection. Under the influence of mass-indignation and the Marxist doctrine we posit a dialectic in history leading on to a Soviet paradise. Arnold Toynbee, half-aware that his study of history still proposes a cyclicism, and half-aware that biblical thought proclaims forwardness, tries to combine the two views: the cyclicisms are the wheels of a convey-ance which carries the true faith; [45] but the metaphor only hides the contradiction, it does not resolve it. These distortions see man as his own god, and history either as man's work or as a naturalism. Nevertheless they obliquely acknowledge the biblical view, namely, that history has a certain forwardness. But the Bible speaks of the Divine encounter, not of an empty "prog-ress." [46]

V

Now a determinative word: Bible history is focused history. The forwardness climbs to a lighted hilltop, and all history be-yond that point is in that light, moving on to the fulfillment of the light. The focal point is Christ; and the lighted hilltop, though the light is darkness, is Calvary. There are three events in Bible history: the Creation, the Christ Event, and the coming "day of the Lord." The Bible makes no apology for this faith: it proclaims it with boldness and remorse and rapture. When our modern mind asks, "But why choose Christ?" the Bible answers, "Men did not choose Christ. Rather they have hurried him to some new Cross in every generation. He chose them, as in every contrite pondering of Him He chooses us." When our modern mind asks, "But why take one event long ago and far away as the clue to history?" the Bible answers, "Why not, if it finds us? Why assume that truth is in a logical syllogism, scien-tific formula, general law, or philosophical abstraction?" There is a certain existentialism about scripture, for it is a book of history. It truckles to our universalisms no more than do the stars or tides. This fact compounds the daringness of the Bible. How could anyone find it dull? Our dreary factualisms are dull. Our so-called "universal laws" are dull, cancelling the vividness of the event in favor of a deadly sameness. Our political conventions are dull, filled with windbag clichés. Our divorce is dull, and our industrialism with its chimney smoke smudges out both landscape and life. But the Bible is not dull. It may be incredible, a wild dream, a madness, and an ecstasy, but it is not tedious: a flash of light, rather, and a spurt of blood—blood of God in our human flesh!

The Bible thus sets a Year One in the midst of history. Every time we date a letter we acknowledge the birth of a Galilean "long ago and far away." Emperors before his time and after tried to make a new calendar, each with his own birth, of course, as the new beginning. They failed, but a lowly man who refused the temptation of the kingdoms of the world, and asked nothing of our earth except the joy and agony of doing what he called "the will of my Father," [47] succeeded, never coveting success, where emperors failed. The correspondence of President Kennedy with Premier Khrushchev, and the dated page of every newspaper, unwittingly pay tribute to a King who refused to be king. Why? Is he both in our world and over against our world in judgment and mercy? Is he the thrust into history of a cauterizing and healing Silence? We cannot analyze Calvary. It is too late, for it has pierced us. That, at least, is the outright avowal of Bible history. Redemption through a person accents the Biblical conviction that history as a whole must be construed through persons, not through "movements" or "patterns." Somewhere is the story of a village green being bought as site for a shortwave radio station. The stone cross which had stood there for centuries had to be moved. It was deep set, and workmen found the task hard. Then the village idiot came (nice touch in the story), saw the struggle of the workmen, and began to sing in an idiot chant: "They can't pull it over. They can't dig it up! It's from the beginning. It's the core of creation." [48]

This focus of history is, to the Bible, the locus of history's redemption. Modern man, after trying for years to believe that history is somehow its own cure, as in the bromide, "Give the race another million years!" now despairs of history. Camus con-

26

jectures that all history may be "absurd," and in the novel entitled *The Fall* would tell us that man is not only "fallen," but must lie hopeless where he falls.[49] Robert Penn Warren says in almost stark despair: "There's no forgiveness for our being human." [50] Hopelessness is but another name for slow death. But in the New Testament there is no *in memoriam* word. History is promise, and the event of Christ is both the fulfillment of the promise and its renewal in a brighter hope. Each age in the Christian story construes this redemption in its own terms. To the Gospel of Mark the Cross is the scene of battle where Christ is victor-victim over Satanic powers. To the Hebrew mind in the early Church Christ is the Atoning Lamb: the metaphor now is not battle, but altar sacrifice. In the age of Roman law, Christ saves men from judgment condemnation: the metaphor is a lawcourt. What of our time? Perhaps our age is so broken that it lacks both style and form, yet our very brokenness may provide the metaphor. Perhaps psychiatry may suggest the symbol. Thus T. S. Eliot's *The Cocktail Party*.[51] Thus Paul Tillich's repeated use of the word "acceptance." [52] At any rate Bible history is history focused in the redemption given in Christ and His Cross.

VI

Once more—this being the culmination—the Bible, being a book of history, presents history as redeemed but not yet redeemed. That is to say, history in the eyes of scripture is in tension, held in polarity between two worlds, the world of men and the mystery of God. It *is* redeemed. Once in a public park at Jacksonville, Florida, we heard another spectator of a chess game say of a certain move, "That's it!" He meant that though the other contestant might squirm for a time, even for a long time, that one move had determined the outcome. The rivals might not know the victorious import of that move, and the other spectators might not know, but that particular onlooker knew: "That's it!" The Bible plays the role of that one perceptive man. By faith, faith being response to the beckoning and

27

grasp of the Mystery, the Bible says of the total Christ Event in history: "That's it!" God has made a final move in our human story, and His word in Christ "shall not return unto [Him] void." [53] But history is not yet redeemed. Many are blind to Christ, and some outrightly oppose him. Even the Church harbors those who do not know that the move has been made, Christ being for them only one more man making one more guess, though with more compassion. In any event the transience and guilt of history can be healed only from beyond history. Therefore history, though redeemed, is not yet redeemed.

So, says the Bible, we in our day live in "the time being," [54] in a strange interim between an accomplished act of God in Christ and its final validation. History in its whole sweep is tension and polarity: caught between two worlds. What a startling and daring view of man's life on this planet! Yet do we not find here true reflection of our own experience? If God is not in Christ, then the best in our earth is finally at the mercy of the worst, and we still know the difference; but if God is in Christ the victory is not yet ratified. We ourselves are still guilty, that fateful choice still bedeviling the drama of man; and there is generation by generation the entail "of man's first disobedience"; yet Light has pierced our pilgrimage, Light in which all time becomes one time. Thus Paul Tillich: "Christian interpretation of history is possible only on the basis of . . . a sacramental element—Christ, the center of history, has come; and a prophetic element—Christ, the end of history, is coming." [55]

So the Bible ends, in what seems to be a providential overruling of the order of the books in the canon, with a picture of the Church crying, "Maranatha": "Even so, come, Lord Jesus!" [56] What other book would dare that ending? The Church knew that Jesus is Lord, the beginning, center, and end of history; and he had come. But they were beset by persecution at the hand of a pagan empire, encompassed by a culture that knew not Christ, and there was treachery in the very midst of the Church. So they cried in tension, in hope fulfilled and hope yet to

28

be fulfilled, in the polarity which is the very nature of history: "Maranatha!" In that tautness they gathered to a Sacrament which showed forth "the Lord's death till he come," [57] and were already at home.

VII

In this chapter we have not wished to argue or even to plead, but rather simply to trace and describe the Bible stance regarding the veiled and unveiled secret called history. In subsequent pages we shall explore the Bible claim. But at long last there is no proof by argument, for when have argument and debate (exercise of the rational or merely logical mind) ever brought conviction? Charles Frankel has said of the historian's task, in a sentence the more striking as coming from a scholar who has written on *The Faith of Reason*,[58] that "Indeed, over and above the explanations an historian gives, whether 'common-sensical' or 'scientific,' we want him to tell a story well and make it come to life." [59] Oh, that last phrase, "come to life"! The Bible is itself history, though not "objective history," for there is no such animal. The Bible is the story of man under the Mystery, and of man's response in faith and doubt, obedience and disobedience, guilt and contrition, calamity and hope. It is history incredibly yet flamingly focused in Christ. It is history redeemed yet not redeemed, history itself looking beyond history to a "Lamb slain from the foundation of the world." [60] Does it tell the story well? Does it "make it come to life"—to your whole life and mine, the Mystery of God visiting the mystery of our total self?

CHAPTER II

The Focus of History

HAS HISTORY ANY FOCUS? DOES IT CARRY ANY MEANING? THE MAN in the street, his naïve faith in progress shattered by two world wars, answers, "Who knows?" He does not know. So he seeks refuge in the amenities of present culture, or he becomes a cynic gentle or cruel, or he "forgets it all" in the activisms of business and politics, or he sidetracks the question for the merry-go-round of a "good time." But the question keeps coming back: "Has history any focus?" If, in Reinhold Niebuhr's striking phrase, history is only "the confusion of spots on the cards used by psychiatrists in a Rorschach test," [1] and if there is no psychiatrist, if history has no meaning, then the life of the man in the street has no meaning. He reads Spengler's account of endlessly cyclic cultures,[2] and asks if that is history: does the music go round and round on a hurdy-gurdy out of tune until the stars are cold? Toynbee's plea that history is an alternation, first the thrust of a new civilization and then the creative acceptance of its demise,[3] stirs him; but not for long, for he asks what is the end of it all, and what becomes of him, John Doe, the man in the street?

Has history any focus? This lonely man, more lonely because he is in the street, opens the morning paper. There is a new crisis in Africa or Berlin: "Raving politics, never at rest!" [4] A tidal wave has killed hundreds in Japan; man cannot trust even the stage called nature on which he struts his part. Behind these major items called "news," though they are not new, a foghorn sounds off Nantucket, a wedding is celebrated in Mexico City, a car skids on an icy road in New Hampshire, and a tubercular child coughs in a Bombay slum. Multiply these happenings back

30

through the millennia to the cave man and beyond, multiply them forward to a planet become too cold or destroyed by a bomb far too hot, and—what sense does it make? Is this a drama? There are no acts or scenes, much less a plot. Is history sheer happenchance?

But every man inquires about the meaning of history. That is to say, every man stands above history. He may exclaim about "the whole blind welter," but by that very phrase he sees it "whole," and he could not say "blind" if he had not first known sight, or "welter" if he had not first glimpsed some plan. There is some kind of focus in the man himself who, though caught in history, is yet able to survey it. Sometimes he is cynical, saying, history is a coral reef, lifted for a moment above uncaring tides, composed of dead insects who think themselves better than insects. Sometimes he is reverent, and prays, "O Thou, . . . before whose Face the generations rise and pass away." [5] He must have some answer to his question about history, for his life is involved, and a life without meaning is drawn-out death. So we ask again, Has history any focus or meaning? We shall seek the clue in the man himself, for all history is centrally the story of men.

I

This first: every historian, meaning any man since we are all historians, takes some stance, and cannot help it. There is no "objective history." For that matter, there is no "objective science": our sciences by their very method reflect our present purposes, which are to fulfill rational mind and extend possessive control. The rock on which all positivisms break is the positivist, for he is always more than analytic mind. The Achilles heel, or the saving grace, of all science is the scientist, for his self goes to far deeper ground than his science. Our humanisms try vainly to deny this verity. For instance, John Dewey in his *Logic* writes: "To be intellectually 'objective' is to discount and eliminate merely personal factors in the operations by which a conclusion is reached." [6] But John Dewey is still the author. Personal factors may be discounted (though why?), but they cannot be elim-

31

inated. The eye is not a camera, nor the ear a recording machine, nor the mind a tape on which the record is made. Existentialism makes its rightful protest against this sterilizing of the subject, in so violent a protest that existentialism may run to the other extreme and try to cancel out the object. None of us can flee either fatefulness or decision.

The "objective" historian sometimes tries to defend his alleged objectivity by taking a tiny patch of our human story, such as a ship's log for one day's journey, or one week in the recorded annals of an old town, and offering it as "hard facts." But such a historian has not eliminated subjectivity. He has *chosen* the patch which actually cannot be torn from the garment, he has *assumed* that the proper manner of dealing with facts is chronological instead of by means of "flashback," and furthermore he has ceased to be historian and become merely scribe. There is no "bare chronicle." Every historian writes from his own nature, his own date, and his own culture. He *selects* his material from a vast array, and the selection involves a faith principle: "I *believe* this is important." He *marshals* his material: "I *believe* this is the organizing center." Is an encyclopedia "objective"? The "Britannica" in the edition I use gives 332 columns to electricity and eleven columns to The Gospel of John. There is no starkly objective history. Benedetto Croce in Italy who, with Wilhelm Dilthey [7] in Germany and R. G. Collingwood in England,[8] pioneered the new mode in the writing of history, claims flatly that all history is "contemporary history." [9] Such an admission, or the milder acknowledgment that history is always a subject-object affair, raises problems, but truth must be accepted whatever problems are raised.

If every historian takes some stance, the main question is, what stance? The Marxist historian takes his stance: he assumes of human nature that matter comes before mind, and that therefore the mind though free is free only to be centrally concerned with matter; and he assumes of history itself that it is an inevitable dialectic. The scientific historian sees cultures as if they were exhibits in a museum, and, being scientific, seeks the clue to human life in the cycles of nature: thus Spengler.[10] The National Association for the Advancement of Colored People has its own view of the history of our Southern states, a view not shared by Governor Faubus. The Hindu sage sees history as a wheel of reincarnations and finds life in the mystic vision. What stance shall we take? There is historical event: an object. We are not dealing with abstractions. No historian has any right to distort the event. Indeed he is under obligation to clarify and validate it. John Calvin is not Billie Sol Estes, and Benedict Arnold is not a Japanese ricksha boy. Historical records are not to be treated as if they were letters by which historians may play a game of scrabble, each making what words he chooses. But though we must be "true to the facts," no man can escape interpretation of the facts. What interpretation? The calendar shows the Christian stance: Christ has split history into before and after.

II

Next: the historian must take some inner stance. He views the past in some chosen attitude or spirit. For history is the story of people like ourselves, even though the very word history, wearing a disguise of academic neutrality, may distract us from that fact, or trick us into dealing with past folk as if they were merely objects. By the words attitude and spirit we mean more than cultural stance. That indeed is an inescapable coloration, and Karl Mannheim has rightly called attention to "the infiltration of the social position" of the historian.[11] Alfred Tennyson, always the country gentleman, dismissed the French Revolution as "the red fool-fury of the Seine," [12] while Wordsworth's comment on the same event was "Bliss was it in that dawn to be alive!" [13] The social milieu of each man, and even his local station and friendships, shaped, though they did not necessarily determine, his verdict. But by "attitude" is here meant individual spirit, humaneness, for instance, or dispassion. John Masefield saw posterity with gentle feeling:

Red helpless little things will come to birth,
And hear the whistles going down the line,
And grow up strong and go about the earth,
And have much happier times than yours and mine.[14]

Should we view the past as a complexity of "actions," or as "social movements," or as "war," or with a mind open to its personal tragedies and hopes? For instance, and it is only instance, how shall we think of the people who were compelled to build the pyramids? That is the question, and what a question!

Thus we may classify historians. Some are curious, easily caught by details that strain credulity, and the not-unworthy result is Ripley's "Believe It or Not." Some look with a cynical eye: they see the depravity rather than the glory, instead of seeing both; and then there is a debunking of history. Some see cause for satire, as when S. Parkes Cadman said wryly of our human story that he had reached the conclusion that our planet is being used as the lunatic asylum of the solar system,[15] though that word assumes that his eyes were sane. The culture pattern school of Melville J. Herskovits views man in history as victim of his culture, and tells us that the victory always goes to the big battalions:[16] an attitude that gives no account of how cultures originate and change, still less of Professor Herskovits' power to stand above cultures to appraise them. Karl Marx had eyes of fierce compassion for the dispossessed, an attitude that gave his writing a measure of truth not to be found in his arbitrary theories. J. H. Green in his *Short History of the English People* forsook the customary account of kings and battles, thus proving himself a democrat and a man of fellow-feeling. So what attitude?

The question now involves the innermost motive of the historian, his hopes and fears, his frustrations and his valor; in short, his credo about our life. A prosecuting attorney proposes a motive for the crime, for if the accused man has no motive he is insane and so not subject to charge. The historian also asks, consciously or unconsciously, about the people of the past, "What moved them?" With that question the historian's own life is instantly involved. He betrays some doctrine of human nature. What doctrine? The historian is granted no immunity, no neutralism, no balcony view. The New Testament says flatly, not least to the historian, "Let this mind be in you, which was also in Christ Jesus." [17] Dr. E. H. Carr in his *What Is History?* [18]—a provocative book, illuminating in its tracing of the influence of social forces in history, but strangely unaware that liberalistic hopes for man's "evolution" have been broken—takes issue with Professor Trevor-Roper's dictum that the historian "ought to love the past," [19] and brands the proposal a "romanticism." Yes, such a verdict could be romantic and even sentimental. But the love of Christ for people was neither, and it could be the only realism.

III

Now to an issue which has already been broached and which is as wide as the board: the historian must look for history's redemption. "Must" is used in no coercive sense. We do not propose that the historian is under obligation to discuss redemption, for that is not his central task. No, he should tell a story well, and make it come to life. What we mean is that the tragedy and brokenness of history, which surely no man can miss, must raise at the back of the historian's mind the immemorial question of man's deliverance; and that sometimes the background question comes to the "front, center, spotlight" of the stage. Nature, which is the locale of history, itself has lesions, as witness "The Black Plague" or the eruption of Vesuvius which buried Pompeii in lava. As for human nature, it is both beset and indwelt by enmities which bring every towering dream to disappointment. These lesions and contradictions are in the historian himself. Meanwhile death comes on, "and after that comes judgment." [20] How can the historian escape the sense of tragedy in our human story?

Some deny that such questions are the historian's concern. Thus Professor W. H. Walsh: "The question whether history has a meaning . . . is extra-historical, just as the question whether nature is intelligible . . . is extra-scientific." [21] But the scientist assumes intelligibility in nature; and, speaking now quite sharply, the realm of nature is not parallel with the realm of history. For nature is object, while man is subject-object; and if man's life has no prime meaning there is no history and nature is a curse. The new view among historians admits this deeper concern. So Benedetto Croce: "Thus if contemporary history springs straight from life, so too does that history which is called noncontemporary, for it is evident that only an interest in the life of the present can move one to investigate past fact." [22] The historian, even as he writes, is himself caught in the dilemmas of history. This Dr. R. G. Collingwood outrightly admits: "It is the historian himself who stands at the bar of judgment, and there reveals his own mind in its strength and weakness, its virtues and vices." [23] Dr. Arnold J. Toynbee, writing of current history, flatly uses the word "salvation": "Along what path are we to look for salvation in this parlous plight . . . ?" [24] But, of course, man's plight on this planet has always been parlous; and behind all writing of history there is the question expressed or unexpressed: How did they find or not find deliverance? We are not saying that such a question should become explicit in the historian's craft: only that it is always implicit, and that in our chosen theme we must openly confront it. We would go further: great writing of history is great drama, and great drama leads on to the great issues of theology.

IV

So we ourselves now come to grips with history's sickness, as every historian must do, covertly if he is content to tell a tale, overtly if he has a compassionate stance and spirit. There is what Herbert Butterfield has called "a gravitational pull" [25] in all historical movement. The drag would be evident even if men did not act the fool. Every advance in knowledge, especially in scientific knowledge, leaves textbooks and those who wrote them out-of-date, so that the wake of the vessel is pathos. Every improvement in technics spells loss and painful readjustment.

The automobile was no blessing to men who raised horses or built horse carriages. Man's building is not only at the mercy of time and nature, as witness the ruins on the Acropolis, but it defeats itself, so that the new suburbs cause an "inner-city blight." Spengler is manifestly right in his contention that cultures decay, as trees decay, as men decay.[26] The downward drag finds its most tragic expression in the fact of death. No man escapes it, with its forerunner of infirmity and its aftermath of sorrow and all the

> Fallings from us, vanishings;
> Blank misgivings of a Creature [27]

which are history's fate. The smell of decay, whatever the renewals, haunts the whole panorama of man's life.

Add the fact of man's culpable folly, and history's sadness is compounded. Sin is not necessarily the breach of the moral code, though such a spoilation is usually involved, for noble people break good codes from above them, as when Jesus defied the Sabbath law for works of healing. No, sin is drawing "a circle premature" [28] to make a god of man and his works. It erects an idol of cash or flesh or status or empire, in the endemic pride which proposes a self-cure for man's anxiety. Sin may or may not be inevitable in our human estate; it is surely responsible, as all our judgments of praise and blame imply. By this folly every invention is given good and evil use: an automobile is an ambulance, but also a gangster getaway-car. Every political system both serves and betrays its people: tyrannies and democracies alike propose peaceful and warlike use of atomic power. Every industrial empire is both blessing and curse: the blessing is evident in our electrically lighted homes; the curse can be seen in the anonymity of city streets, the mechanization of the handworker, the threat to creativeness posed by mass production, and the pride of "senior executive status." Idols are man made, and the deliverance which they promise or which their makers attribute to them is therefore always phantasy,

37

and the phantasy leads on to frenzies of "blood and soil." [29]
History is the history of man's fateful and oft abused freedom.

Let us summarize the other particulars in history's clamant
need. History is transient, so that time sweeps away the sound
and the fury, and equally the power and the glory. History is
sometimes irrational, as when Hitlerism sprang from subconscious depths. Yes, there were clear psychological and political
antecedents, but these do not fully explain either the portent
itself or the demonic convergence of forces. History is irrevocable:
Pilate said stubbornly, "What I have written, I have written," [30]
little realizing that the inscription is history's bane. History is
brought to judgment, and no man can gloss the crime or bribe
the law, for history's name is already on the police blotter.
History, the proud and bedraggled pageant of man, cannot re-
deem itself. Time cannot heal it, despite our proverb, for time
brings death. Is not time itself infected? We do not know, but
it is clear that time is not a washing machine with a rotary
flow which gets rid of all the dirt and lint. Thus Paul Tillich's
word that all history, in the writing of it and the living of it,
is the "history of salvation." [31]

V

Where is the salvation? That is the main question. If we can
find an answer, we shall know also the proper stance and spirit.
The answer of Christian faith is not to be dismissed out-of-hand
as "indoctrination," as if academic "neutrality" were not indoctrination, namely, the sheer pretense that human beings can
be neutral. Nor may we honorably label the Christian answer
"escape," for the last proposal to be made about the man crucified is that He was running away from life; it would make
much more sense to say that our glib use of the word "escape"
is our running away from Him. There is no "proof" of Christ,
for He is not in the area of academic argument, but there are certain facts: He has split the calendar into before and after, and
His Cross (worse than a gibbet at the first) is strangely set in
our world—in our finest music and architecture, against the sky-

38

line of every city, and poignantly above our graves. So to our central question.

This much is clear: the redemption of history must be from within history. Yes, from beyond it also, for history is the sickness; yet the cure cannot be by celestial radar, or it would be bafflement crying, "Do they really care out there?"; and perhaps it would be mockery. Redemption must be by transfusion of blood. For true deliverance is not merely cancellation of the past, if that were possible or desirable, but, as any parent knows who has had a wayward child, an outright sharing of life at cost of love. There are deeper reasons why redemption must be from within history. One is this: we cannot be lifted above the human dilemma without our consent, for we have a certain freedom, and we cannot consent unless we see the redeemer busy at the task. Another, more profoundly, is this: the Creation, the mysterious origin of nature and history, is under indictment, in such a question as, "How can God forgive Himself [for cancer and crime] unless God shares our life?" Why cancer and crime come we still may not know, but if God exposes Himself to all "the slings and arrows of outrageous fortune" [32] we can await the answer—or ask no answer because question and answer are now overwhelmed by Divine love. Is Jesus in history? If he is not, if he only mimics our human life, if (to quote bad theology widely current) "he knew all along that he was the Son of God," if thus his temptations were only shadowboxing and his Cross a fiction, he is not redemption, but almost an insult to our pain.

The answer is not far to find. Jesus came as a climax to covenant faith and "chose twelve" (continuance of the twelve tribes?) as faith's continuance. What we are now saying is that he is not an isolated figure, not a man without a country, not a man without a date. His life is woven into history's tapestry. We pause for this comment: the Christological question is not approachable as if he were isolated, and not answerable in long discussions about "the nature of Christ": the problem, if ever

39

it could so be described, is not in the order of nature, but in the order of history; and the answer is not in the logic of our minds, but in the total man through the venture of our will. To return to our journey: the Creeds (which are defense against destructive misinterpretation, not coercive "indoctrination"; banners under which a man may pledge his life, not dreary theological argument) protest any heresy that would make Jesus mere antic or abstraction: "[He] suffered under Pontius Pilate." [33] Thus Christ's date and country. He "was made of a woman, made under the law," [34] sharing our strange freedom, sharing also the constraints of heredity and environment. He hungered and thirsted. He knew frustration: "He could do no mighty work there because of their unbelief." [35]

There could be and should be a further spelling out of the historical reality of Christ. Thus: it is worse than caricature to propose that he lived in "ancient, pastoral calm," and therefore can have no meaning for our chaotic time. For he lived in Belgium during the German occupation—or in Palestine during the Roman occupation. He heard many languages: Greek, which was almost a *lingua franca* across the world from Spain to Northern India, Latin, Hebrew, Aramaic. He stood at the crossroads of empire. He stood with inner pain at the crossroads of decision. Should he join the underground with the Zealots, or become "monastic" with the Essenes (it is nonsense to try to link him with the Qumran community, for he refused that choice), or "virtuous" with the Pharisees, or collaborator with the Sadducees? He turned away from all these options, and trod instead the strange road (as real as the road outside your door) of a Cross (as actual as wood and nails). We should add that he disowned the omniscience which some would falsely ascribe to him ("But of that day or that hour no one knows, not even the angels of heaven, nor the Son, but only the Father"),[36] and bore the burden of our not knowing. The Gospel is not theory, not philosophy, not logic, not at core either theology or science; it is history, event, Person, and community. Yes, Jesus is in history.

40

Yet the redemption of history must come from beyond history, for the whole corpus of history is sick and tragic. Yes, the panorama has animation, or we would not recognize the sickness; and joy, or we would not know "the tragic sense of life." [37] But all history stands in need, as any one man's life in its transience and guilt stands in need. Only the invasion of new life can save history from its endemic idolatries. So we must now ask if Jesus, in history, is also from beyond history. Before answer is made we should be clear as to the terms on which alone answer can be given. There can be no logical proof, for God is not the end term of a syllogism: He is the Axiom in Whom all the axioms on which logic depends find their home. Likewise there can be no scientific proof, for God is not an object to be demonstrated; and, if He were, He would be but another Object, however huge, standing in a roster of objects, and could not be God. No, God is the Eternal Subject. It is strange indeed, and blind, that our generation should demand of faith in Christ "proofs" that could never prove, and evidence that could never convince. If we treated love with that rational shabbiness, that shabby rationalism, there would be no love.

Then what questions should we ask of Jesus if we would know his beyondness? Questions from the whole man addressed to the total Christ Event, not partial questions which both betray and flatter our pride of mind and our clutching emotionalisms. Does Christ convict us of guilt and stir in us a new penitence? This question is almost central, for guilt is not merely self-destructive or antisocial, for we did not and could not create either our own life or our neighbor's: sin is against the Creative Mystery. So, does Christ quicken guilt and penitence, and thus become the thrust of the Mystery? Does He answer in lightning flash or spreading dawn the immemorial questions, "Who am I?" and "Why am I?" The one question inquires about our origin, and its secret earlier form is "Who are you?"; and it can find answer only in light. The latter question inquires about destiny, and again the answer cannot be by argument or from

41

any merely human dialogue, for God is and must be "His own Interpreter." Does Christ answer these questions in the wholeness of Encounter? Does He gather all history into unity, thus redeeming its chaos? Does He give meaning to the otherwise bleak and blank facts of pain and death, answering them not in an "explanation" which could never explain, but in a Cross (convergence of all meaninglessness, pain, and death) which breaks in light? Does He speak grace to our blunderings, and grant our total life a new purpose which is in the earth, never seeking escape, yet not of the earth?

These questions, standing on "the border" where man both views his own life and becomes aware of the Unconditioned Life, almost shout their own joyous "Yes!" Accounts of the Virgin Birth and of the Resurrection bristle with difficulties, a fact which only ignorance of the Scriptures or equal obduracy can deny. But as life testimony to the impact of Christ on the wholeness of man's person they kindle and flame. As for the doctrine of the Virgin Birth, the testimony says: "He is not of transience only, not merely of human lineage, not locked in our inconclusive series of births and deaths." As for the Resurrection, it cries aloud from the lips and life of men who had been surprised by Joy, that Christ is not victim of our funeral processions, but was born of the Holy Spirit and was raised from death by God's sovereign power. He laid on men the demand and succor of the Unconditioned. He refused any part of our idolatries, asking no fame, no wealth, no comfort of home, no solace of marriage, no monument, no army, no status. Nay, he asked no "righteousness" of the kind which in us easily becomes self-righteousness: "Why do you call me good?", he asked: "No one is good but God alone." [38] That is why we call him good!—both because he asked the question and gave the answer, and because in that lowliness we are grasped in our total self by the Divine. His not coveting gives him a point of vantage beyond all our power structures and idolatries, and he thus becomes judgment; his sharing of our need gives him point of vantage within our world, and he thus becomes our mercy. When

42

we bring real questions to him, the needle of our total life swings to him quiveringly, and then settles, as a compass to the magnetic north.

VI

Yes, this verdict about Christ is by faith. We need not apologize for that confession, but offer it as bold avowal. For faith is always response, as a man is waylaid by Mystery. Moreover all writing of history is faith response. This verdict holds even of the positivist approach to history, with its dreary empiricisms and its endless probing of such words as "explanation" and "cause" as they relate to historical study. There is some rigor in this new scholasticism,[39] just as in setting-up exercises. But the faith behind these inquiries is, "truth is empiricism," a proposition that could never be empirically proved; and setting-up exercises, whatever their conceded value, are not the fatefulness of history or the onset and decision of our daily life. Yes, this view of Christ is by faith—our response in the whole man to being grasped by the Christ Event. Says Paul Tillich: "History cannot be understood from the outside. . . . All historical interpretation contains a concrete historical decision; that is, the spectator's point of view has been abandoned." [40] Yes, "has been" if only in the decision which says, "I will pretend that I am a spectator, not involved in life."

The faith of a follower of Christ holds that Christ is the focus of history, even as he has split the calendar of history into before and after; that he is the stance from which the panorama should be viewed, and the spirit in which it should be viewed. That is to say, a historian should "love the past," though only in the realism of the love of Christ. We cannot enter deeply into "the thoughts" of men in other ages, despite R. G. Collingwood's repeated prescription,[41] except as they and we alike are held in Christ as the re-creative center of all human story; and still less can we have empathy with nature, as Croce astonishingly proposed: "Do you wish to understand the history of a blade of grass? First and foremost, try to make yourself into a blade of grass." [42] I tried, and found myself scampering at the very sight of a lawn mower. But even that demand as to nature is not utterly strange if a man says of Christ, the Eternal Logos, "All things were made through him." [43] For this high faith, Christ is the center of history. He, not the invention of printing, for it brought pornography, as well as the poetry of John Keats. He, not the Renaissance, for it dwindled into the dreary questionings of the Enlightenment, as that into our *Age of Anxiety*.[44] He, not the discovery of nuclear power, for it may end in nuclear death. The center of history is the Event which is both Judgment and Mercy, which stands between land and sea—the land on which the drama of history is enacted, and the mysterious sea along which we walk and across which we gaze asking "Is there any word from the Lord?" [45]

VII

There is a story of a philosopher who was asked in an ancient time why he came to the Olympics. He replied that some came to compete, others to buy and sell, and a third group simply to look on; and added that he was of the third group. Francis Bacon, commenting on the story, said, "It is reserved only for God and angels to be lookers on." [46] As for the work of angels, Milton would have us believe that they "post o'er land and ocean without rest." [47] As for God, we do not know with our minds alone, though we can hardly escape the surmise that if He is the eternally Passive Spectator, he could not be God. God in Christ carried a heavy cross up a bleak hill. No man can merely "look on" in history, and the meaning of history is always hidden from neutral eyes. "All historical interpretation contains a concrete historical decision." [48] The decision is an answer to the question: "What do you think of the Christ?" [49] History is Dialogue between God and man-in-pilgrimage in the language of Event; and Christ is the Conversation's middle term, the key to the translation, the light in which the whole pilgrimage can be seen and understood, and the love in which history's brokenness is healed.

44

CHAPTER III

History and Progress

IS THE WORLD GETTING BETTER? ILLUMINATING QUESTION! IT IM-
plies that though we have heretofore accepted the Biblical view
of a certain "forwardness" in history, we now begin to wonder
if the "forwardness" is betterment, or if there is any real movement. We have taken for granted that history ought not to be
static or cyclic, for human beings ought not to be sentenced to
fixity or to a squirrel cage, but we now ask, "Can we take it for
granted?" There has been a contest as to the meaning of history
between "your sons, O Zion" and "your sons, O Greece";[1] and
Zion with its interpretation of history as Dialogue and pilgrimage
has thus far won over Greece with its interpretation of history
as an endless circle. But now we question the victory: "Is the
world getting better?" Perhaps history, despite its "infinite
variety," is as fixed and constricted as a child's kaleidoscope;
perhaps it is a squirrel cage or an endless wheel; perhaps it is
illusion.

The question is strange and illuminating in another sense: we
ask it as spectators, without any sharp piercings of conscience.
We assume a Godlike pose as we survey two vast realms, history
and progress. But we are not gods. For, though we can survey
history, we are also involved. We are shaped by history, but history is also (to use Heidegger's plea) our responsible burden.[2]
Thus the question, "Is the world getting better?", should be
followed and overcome in another question, "Am I getting
better?" What further questions that question raises, not least
questions about self-righteousness, and questions about the mean-

ing of "better"! In any event, it is a safe guess that the issue of history and progress has never been more urgently raised than in our time, and perhaps never with graver misgivings.

I

The pendulum has swung from optimism to pessimism in hardly more than a generation. Usually a whole epoch is needed to bracket such a sweeping change, but some of us have seen the extremes spanned within a lifetime. As to the optimism, Ralph Waldo Emerson in his Andover Hall Address compared man with the idyllic June days during which he spoke.[3] There was no mention of snakes in the grass, germs in the air, or thunderbolts in the sky. Man also was not too far from paradise. All he needed was an essay called "Self-Reliance." [4] Then he would prove himself another Christ, and proceed to write another Bible. Perhaps the essay was unwitting forerunner of our aggressive commercialism and our political plundering! In that same era Mark Twain expressed the wish that Walt Whitman, then seventy, might live for another thirty years, for then he would see man "at almost his full stature at last!" [5] He echoed Condorcet, who wrote a full century earlier that "no bounds have been fixed to the improvement of human faculties; that the perfectibility of man is absolutely indefinite; and that the progress of this perfectibility, henceforth above the control of every power that might wish to halt it, has no other limit than the duration of the globe upon which nature has placed us." [6] The Crystal Palace was built in London [7] with Condorcet *bravura*, and dedicated to perpetual peace: men had become too civilized ever again to indulge the barbarities of war. Incidentally the Palace burned soon after, falling into a crumpled wreck. But this, and a worse human holocaust, men could not then foresee: it was a fair and ample time.

Now we are pessimists, and we do not ask if our pessimism has any more substance than the earlier hope. Our book titles are eloquent of our despair. Jean Paul Sartre writes of life as *Nausea*

46

and *No Exit.*[8] Despite my own indebtedness to him for a certain realism, I cannot overcome the suspicion that he is enjoying his brave misery. Albert Camus describes our planet as a plague-stricken city with all lines of communication cut: thus his *The Plague.*[9] Elsewhere he outrightly proposes that all life is "absurd."[10] W. H. Auden writes, though from the angle of a deeper hope, of *The Age of Anxiety,*[11] picturing our generation as a group of people getting slowly drunk in a tavern, each talking about himself interminably—tubercular folk seeking cure by breathing into one another's faces. As final verge there is a book title: *Modern Man Is Obsolete.*[12] More thoughtfully, Karl Löwith, in an acute survey of theories of history, and therefore more strikingly, writes, "Man's historical experience is one of steady failure . . . only our means of oppression and destruction (as well as of reconstruction) are considerably improved and adorned with hypocrisy."[13]

Some see abatement of the pessimism. Sartre finds it in the courage to walk into nothingness.[14] But can there be such courage? The word courage comes from the Latin *cor*, meaning heart. What man can have heart for nothingness? He can smother his heart in a dull stoicism perhaps, and so live, but he will not know the zest of courage. Dr. E. H. Carr, on the other hand, finds hope in the revolutionary movements of our time.[15] He proclaims himself incorrigible optimist. Our base mood, he says, comes from what Spengler described as *The Decline of the West:*[16] we would not be pessimists if we lived in the surge of the East. But surely this is a whistling in the dark. The East has monolithic tyrannies, brainwashings, and appalling "liquidations." Moreover, what when the East declines? Most people nowadays find no relief from current gloom: they live in noisy distraction or quiet desperation. Reinhold Niebuhr quotes H. G. Wells as example of despair following undue hope: "A frightful queerness has come into life. . . . The writer is convinced that there is no way out, or around, or through the impasse. It is the end."[17]

II

Why was the Victorian time so confident? Why do we question its assumptions? Because of the stern logic of recent events. Then what fallacies have events revealed in the earlier hope? Answer to these questions may lead to realism, and the realism may encourage us to ask if our despair has any more solid substance. So let us swiftly summarize.

They of the hopeful time tended to equate the processes of nature with the discontinuous, not parallel processes of history. The word growth betrayed them. Trees grow, seeded fields come to harvest, and a child's body develops into the frame of a man. Therefore (it was a false "therefore") man's mind grows into ever-fuller knowledge and his spirit into brotherly love. Even if the analogy were valid, it carried its own denial; for trees also die, sometimes in a storm that shows worms at the trunk's core; and harvest fields sometimes suffer blight, and always in northern climes they come into winter's icy hand; and manhood's frame sickens to the grave. It is interesting to note that the optimist points to "growth" in nature, while the pessimist points to nature's decay. Actually nature is cyclic, with both growth and decay. Nature is "object," and therefore "scientific" views of history (even Arnold J. Toynbee does not completely escape them) always end in cyclicism. Churches which hold summer conferences, with accent on the summer and on vesper services fronting the sunset, stress the growth and so become blind to the decay. They rightly thank God for beauty on hill and meadow. But they ignore the coming blizzard. Therefore they encourage the modern nonsense of, "I can worship God better in the country." A quacking duck may there punctuate a man's prayers; and, as for me, I have never met a duck that could quack devotionally.

But, of course, the analogy with nature, interpreted whether in optimism or pessimism, is not valid. History is the record of man rather than of nature.[18] History tells of act-ual-ities, events

48

set in man's unpredictable freedom. Thus Christian faith is a historical faith, not a nature ritual. In the very first century, it took sharp issue with the mystery cults and their stock-in-trade, the celebration of the dying-and-reviving year. There is a certain automism in nature: harvests must grow and fade. But man does not necessarily grow in goodness: he can blacken the human harvest, and even destroy the mortal ground of his life. Thus the analogy is not only false, but it leads on to death-in-optimism and to death-in-despair. A printer explained how type is now set by light rays (nature's boon), and in the next breath spoke of a man whose unruliness was bedeviling the whole shop. Nature and human nature are in different dimensions: a tree cannot be compared with a trauma. The Bible does indeed speak of growth, but its plea is for growth in wisdom (the granting of eternal wisdom) and growth in grace (the given grace of God's love).

There was another fallacy: recent optimism borrowed from the Darwinian concept of evolution to assume an evolution in man. Dr. E. H. Carr frequently uses this word, even after warning us that we must not regard history as something with a capital H.[19] This fallacy is variant of the false comparison between nature and human nature. Even supposing the evolution analogy were true, there are locked types in Darwinian theory. Are people also locked in adult childishness or ultraconservatisms in our ever changing world? Besides, there are reversions to type. Do people also revert, as in Hitler's "blood and soil"?[20] Besides, there are in Darwinian theory the "survival of the fittest" and the multitudinous death of the unfit. Is that the true picture of man's story? There is no hope in the borrowing of the word "evolution." Meanwhile its meaning changes—and changes. It is not now an escalator, but a series of kangaroo leaps; or by Lloyd Morgan's description,[21] it both emerges and evolves; or, in more modern theory, there is an unpredictable newness in every new event.

But, by whatever theory, "evolution" cannot be posited of human nature. If evolution has inevitability is man really free, or

49

is he merely a dummy riding an escalator? If, on the other hand, man has a measure of genuine freedom, can he not wreck the escalator (or any other "evolution"), as when the obscurantist denies to the scientist his proper liberty, or a white mob threatens Negro children enrolling in an integrated school? If there is an unpredictable newness in every new event, should we ever say of Christian faith that it "came from" animism? Even for science the rightful phrase is "arose in," and for Christian faith it is "sent by": "There was a man sent from God whose name was John." [22] Our own awareness knows that man, while he is in nature, also stands above it, even to the strange power to view his own life. In that self-transcendence man is lifted above all evolutionary types, though by his freedom he may sink into them —locked or given to reversion.

There was a further fallacy, still rife in our time: Victorian optimism borrowed from an untenable Greek estimate of man's reason. To the Greeks, perhaps from as far back as Orphic times, reason was "divine," a pure ray of light from the eternal *Logos*. The "soul" (reason) is imprisoned in the body. *Soma* (flesh), they said, is *sema* (prison). This view persists, especially in universities. It infects the Church, which then proceeds to "save men's souls," as if their hands and eyes were worthless, and as if the "soul" could be sent to heaven beforehand by American Express. But sharp questions must be asked about reason. Is it simple? No, it is complex, with subconscious depths and self-transcendent powers. Is it "up there," presiding over the body? No, it is both "up there" and "down here," and being "down here" it is entangled with the rest of life, so that a tiny medical injection can submerge it in a blackout. Is it pure light? No, it can be prostitute to evil cause.

These answers should be explored in depth, and would be here if they were central in our theme, for they are almost momentous in the whole field both of education and of life.[23] Here we can add only a brief comment. Reason is *not simple:* it has strata on strata, and the self with which it is involved is still more

50

complex, so complex as to have within it multiple dialogues, not to mention its dialogues with other selves and with the Mystery. Reason is *not separate*: it is permeated with emotion, so that even philosophy by the very meaning of the word is the love of wisdom; and it is inextricable from the will, for laboratory tests have shown that thought is always incipient action. Reason is *not pure*:

> What damned error but some sober brow
> Will bless it, and approve it with a text.[24]

Here reason ("sober brow") perverts even the Bible to promote error and violence, as in the instance of "white citizens' councils" in our South. The reason can become idolatrous, that is to say, absolutized, as in our word "Learning," spoken almost with bated breath. Why a university? For the sake of "Learning" (all kneel). The word stands there, a verb form without either subject or object. Learning by whom? The question is not asked: man is a hopper waiting for "learning," and if his reason is sufficiently exercised, he can be trusted to act reasonably. Learning what? It does not much matter: anything so long as it is learning. Biblical faith never sells out to this idolatry. Its pages have no trace of anti-intellectualism, but it warns always against pride of mind. The Victorian age exalted reason almost to a heavenly stance. The reason could solve every mystery at last. For particulars see our American trust in progress, or some professor's naïve idea that reason is a pure light above our human scene, which always chooses the creative path from a roster of clear alternatives! Dr. Carr in the book already cited is still caught in this idolatry, for he uses the word "reason" as hopefully as the word "evolution." [25]

We cite one other fallacy of the erstwhile optimism (though it does not exhaust the list): its borrowing from philosophic universalism. Here we confront so vast a portent that we can but instance. Thus we point to the phrase, "the progress of the race."

51

Every individual must die, but the race advances. But how can the race finally advance if every individual dies? There can be social ameliorations meanwhile, but ultimately? Yes, history in its writing must be concerned with social forces. Arnold Toynbee in his monumental work [26] (it is monumental to our gain, despite the blind spots) is in turn historian, sociologist, and at last theologian; and this surely is a valid option. As for social forces, whether labeled "race" or by some other name, history is more than "the shadow of great men," for they are the product as well as the guidance of their time. Karl Marx was not "the criminal father of the Russian Revolution" as many bromides from many chambers of commerce would have us believe, for only millions of men can make a world revolution. Marx was carried on a tide, and in that movement gave the tide an articulation which cannot bear scrutiny. Our sociologies are boon to a clearer understanding of history. But they cannot dismiss the individual.

"The progress of the race" may become almost a monstrous phrase, for it may annihilate the individual. The writing of history is always tempted to that callousness. Morton White would have us believe that history is but a branch of sociology.[27] He helps us to see the inescapable social cast in the historian's craft. But he himself writes as an individual and his argument breaks on that fact. Meanwhile the individual, as in his own fine instance, has a power to view life, a power not given to a crowd or society or race: only a lonely man can speak the perceptive and prophetic word. If he is to be ploughed under age after age for the sake of a race which is always arriving but never arrives, what meaning can we ever hope to find in human story? Is the race blessed, can it be blessed, if its alleged progress is at the price of contempt for even one crippled child? Toynbee's proposal that Christian faith is carried on the wheels of dying civilizations has this unwitting callousness.[28] If the human wheels consent to the plan, there is decency and even glory. But if they do not know, history is indecent, for then it involves wholesale contempt for human life. "The progress of the race!" Not even Genghis Kahn, with his mountain of human skulls, dreamed of such wholesale "liquidation." Meanwhile what if the planet is growing cold? Meanwhile does the race progress? The Bible proposes no "rugged individualism." But it sees a secret and immeasurable preciousness in every individual life.

We cite but one other instance of this vague universalism: our bland use of the word "freedom," in such phrases as "the free world" or "free enterprise." Victorian optimism was sure that freedom, worth any price, was slowly or swiftly spreading through our world. The free man is the guarantee of what is called "our advancing civilization." Thus Hegel: "It is a result of speculative philosophy that freedom is the sole truth of Spirit." [29] Our version is, "Let Freedom ring!", and only a heartless man could remain unmoved. What Hegel meant by "Spirit" is not clear to me and perhaps was not clear to him; and it is worth noting that the end term of his system was the Prussian state, as it is worth remembering what that violently foisted on our world. If "Spirit" means God, then we must perforce think of God as free, free even in His grace of self-limitation for our sakes; but man is free only in his constituted nature. A fish is free only as a fish: its bony structure and its habitat define its freedom. It cannot fly like an eagle or walk like a man; and if it should leap out of the pond "into a wider world," it would not be free: it would be dead. So (it cannot be said too sharply in our time) freedom is not an ultimate word, for it rests back on questions rarely asked: What is the essential nature and true habitat of the creature called man? Only so, in the terms of that question, can free enterprise or the free world be genuinely free.

Meanwhile—it is central fact in our wholesale trust in "freedom," man can abuse his freedom to become a slave, as witness a drug addict or a political tyrant. We should sing "Let freedom ring"—the more gratefully in a land where a man can speak the rightful word and not fear Gestapo death at night. But we should not equate freedom with uprightness or brotherly love, for freedom may degenerate into license, or even into the freedom to destroy ourselves. Thus Rudolf Bultmann: "Man has to be free from himself or to become free from himself. But man cannot get such freedom by his own will and strength, for in such effort he would remain 'the old man'; he can only receive this freedom as gift." [30] If we were wise we might not brag about freedom: we might see it as a burden too heavy to be borne—alone.

We have tried to trace a few of the fallacies that cankered Victorian optimism. Beneath all of them there was a worse blindness: the resolute refusal to confront the fact of death, not death in the abstract, or death sometime, or somebody else's death, but death for you and me and every other man in history. Thus history's tragic cast, for history (we had better speak bluntly) is a continuous graveyard—unless history is healed from beyond history. Moreover death is compounded by dark irrationalities, convergences of events which drive men and nations into insane action. Easy minds dismiss such words as "tragedy" and "accident" and "demonic" as applied to history, but surely sensitive minds cannot be so glib. Two world wars are not passing clouds above "the progress of the race." Only a callous mind or one seeking escape could look at the prison camp at Dachau,[31] and cry "Excelsior!" Only Rover Boy fiction could picture the last fifty years as man climbing by his own power upward and onward to emancipated mind and the fraternal society. It is better to wake to stinging facts than to sleep with pleasant dreams, for presumably a sleeping man must either wake or die. Our pessimism is true at least in this: it does not shy away from realism.

III

Now we must ask if modern pessimism is also cankered by fallacies. Is history finally frustration? Is it no better than a circling year, with its springtime and winter, lost at last in cosmic silence? Must men forever

> plough the light sand and sow
> Seed after seed, where none can ever grow? [32]

That is our prevailing mood. We ask the questions and answer, "Yes." To Albert Camus, man is Sisyphus.[33] The stone is never

54

rolled to the top of the mountain. Always at some stage it rolls back; its weight overcomes the man, and finally crushes him. So Camus debated general suicide as the only intelligent option for men caught in history. But the Biblical view of history, which these chapters offer uncoercively as a live option, but without any apology, would answer at once: "If hopes were dupes, fears may be liars." [34]

The Biblical proposal is that progress is the wrong word: inappropriate, incongruous, incompatible, mismatched, and irrelevant. You supply the other adjectives: dissentient, inapt, inept, infelicitous, and finally repugnant. For the word progress is on a horizontal line, and human nature is not merely or mainly on that line. Yes, this view is more startling in its own way than any Camus proposal. But, then, the Bible is a startling book. The word "progress" (progressus) means movement forward. But if man is viewed only horizontally, where is the port of departure, and where the port of arrival? They are hidden in the twin mysteries of birth and death. The ship's log advises that the vessel is now a thousand miles east of Nantucket and should arrive at Southampton, winds and tides allowing, on such a day at such an hour. But where is history's Nantucket or Southampton? There are certain guidances from the past, despite those who tell us that we find "values" only as we travel ("values": sainted word nowadays, though when examined it proves to be both polygamous and mercenary). Lincoln's Second Inaugural is guidance from the past; and, by the same token, there may be fairly clear goals ahead, as when a man resolves to graduate cum laude. But these guidances and goals under scrutiny may prove to be better than horizontal. Always we are haunted by two questions: the question of origin ("Who am I?") and the question of destiny ("Why am I?"). There is no answer on the horizontal line. That is why the Bible undercuts the whole question of history and progress, insisting: "Wrong word; false question!" Startling book!

There is this to attest the Bible: whenever we try to measure progress in history, we fail. In individual instances, such as Bene-

55

dict Arnold or Abraham Lincoln, we may be fairly sure about "better" and "worse," though even there some cynic might say: "What's the difference in a nihilistic world?" Moreover these instances may be above and below the horizontal line; that is to say, on another scale of measurement. In broader instances we are left in doubt. Dr. Carr reckons our age "better" because we have outlawed the child labor of an earlier industrial age,[35] but we could cite in rebuttal the millions of children killed in our world wars, together with the fact that an acquisitive society and neglectful parenthood breed maladjustment in children. The optimist pleads that we have risen above primitive savagery; the pessimist quotes the alleged comment of a cannibal on our bombing raids: "What a pity to kill so many when they can eat only a few!" The optimist claims that the automobile has bound friendships and family love in a stronger bond because it has overcome distance; the pessimist points to gangster getaway cars and to mass killings on our highways. How can we be sure of progress or regress when there are no fixed points from which to measure? Said Elijah: "It is enough . . . take away my life; for I am not better than my fathers." [36] He was neither optimist nor pessimist, except for some conviction that he ought to be better, and that history should show improvement in the human creature.

The real trouble with the word "progress" is that inasmuch as it is a word on a horizontal line it can do no justice to man's life either in his loneliness or in the agelong society called history. "Man," says Martin Heidegger, "is that strange creature who can view his own life." [37] That is to say, man lives creatively on a vertical line as it cuts the horizontal. The historian's craft is itself on both lines: he sees as from an upper window the odyssey of man's life on this planet, but is himself agent in the odyssey. On which line shall we measure progress?

> Let us honor if we can,
> The vertical man

Though we value none
But the horizontal one.[38]

If we live at the crux of the two lines so that our days are literally crucial, how can we combine the two measurements? A field can be measured horizontally, but how far is it from the sky? A house can be measured horizontally, but what about a home? It could be argued that there are no fixed points on the vertical line. No, but "up" is heaven, though in no poor slide-rule meaning, and "down" is hell. Light breaks from above, by which we know, for instance, that every other human being lives on a vertical line; and that therefore we cannot "use" him or exploit him, because there is a meaning in him which cannot be horizontally computed. The instruments of the scientist are on the horizontal, but the demand on him not to falsify his findings is on the vertical.

Now we are grappling with real issues: not little questions about horizontal progress, but profound questions about the light that strikes our horizontal journey. One such question is, What is the nature of truth? Truth is not logic, for logic rests back on accepted axioms. Truth is not empiricism: for human beings there is no such thing. Truth is not scientific findings only, for man is more than mind; and the scientist himself knows that full truth is always more than a formula on a page: he himself must be true. To whom? Say to his fellow-scientists and to all men. But to what in them? To that which makes them subjects, not merely objects; in short, to the vertical line. Truth is the light that streams down a vertical line, the bestowal of the Above in which man has already a slim foothold, from which he views his own life. Truth is gift of the Mystery, for without Mystery there could be no meaning. Meaning without Mystery is exactly what we call it—a dead certainty; Mystery without meaning is an equally deadly bafflement and frustration.

Then what is reason? What is central in its complexity? Perhaps the mind is not mainly or centrally philosophical, for philos-

57

ophy deals in abstractions; or scientific, for the measurements of science are on the horizontal line; or even theological, for theology is the needed map, but not the traveled country. No, perhaps the core of reason is historical, that constitutive nerve in us which enables us to respond to the onsets of God in history. Thus E. G. Collingwood writes of his own craft as historian: "It follows that . . . historical thinking is an original and fundamental activity of the human mind, or, as Descartes might have said, the idea of the past is an 'innate' idea." [39] If such a proposal is valid, history taught in depth could become the core of any curriculum; and we would use new adjectives concerning man's reason: not vague, theoretical, generalized adjectives, but such words as "whole," "existential," "practical," "purposeful," "relevant," and "open to the Mystery."

Then how is truth found? It is not found: it finds us. Light strikes through historical event on the historical reason. That is why politics and economics excite us, even to the point of violent controversy, while concepts divorced from life are still dull. That is why sermons applied to life, to laissez-faire commerce, for instance, or our stubborn segregation, always draw outraged cries from the privileged: "Stick to the Gospel!" The cry really means: "Stick to platitudes, and deal with our reason as if it were theoretical!" Then is there one Event which illumines the whole roster of events, and thus becomes the clue to the whole human story? Is there one Event in which the past and the future become present? Biblical faith is a *skandalon*: it finds in the total event of Christ the central crossing of the horizontal line, the Light by which we see both darkness and light in the panorama of history, and the demand by which past and future become present. Dr. Carr ridicules such a claim. God, he says, may not be used as "joker in the pack." [40] The very phrase is a contradiction in terms. If the word God has any meaning, how could He be "joker"? Suppose He makes the pack, and deals it, and sets the rules; and suppose the game is not a game, but life itself in history. Then there is no joker, though there might be Grace.

58

IV

If the word is not "progress," what is the word? We have suggested "ongoingness" or "forwardness," and such a word is necessary to remind us that man is on pilgrimage, an ever new man amid new events. But the word does no justice to the vertical line. As we travel, events are always on two lines. Thus life is always crucial. Electricity, let us say, is the new event. It cuts the horizontal pilgrimage. Thus there is a pit opened beneath the horizontal: electricity can be used to crack a safe or to murder a man. But there is an opening above the horizontal: electricity can be used to guide an airplane through the night or to light a hospital. That upper opening is from above, and is the only line of "progress." But, since it is from above, the word "progress" is poor indeed; the line is by Grace from above and by man's glad obedience from below. If a man obeys once, Grace informs him. But there is no vested interest in virtue. The next new event—a birth, a Cuban crisis, a medical discovery—cuts the pilgrimage, and once more decision must be made. How, then, can history be a closed circle or a guaranteed "progress"? It is a crossing of two lines—in the shape of a Cross! Even the maladjusted adolescent in *Catcher in the Rye* [41] was aware of another line of measurement, for when he was asked what he really wished to do he answered (in pathetic misquoting of the poem) that he would like to be "catcher in the rye": to stand at the top of a cliff to save children from danger. But standing is not progress, and children saved may grow up to be thugs. Yes, but there are other than horizontal lines.

Does someone say that the vertical line is an act of faith? So is any line, not least the line of our alleged progress. Even logic rests back on accepted axioms. But faith is never blind faith: it is response to God's onsets in history—and to the Great Event. "But," someone persists, "a man may misconstrue events." Yes, his self will may intervene in pride of "progress," or he may sink into thinghood and so become blind to the sky, or a prevailing culture may condition him almost solely to the horizontal: "Civilization," says Alan Tate, "is the agreement, slowly arrived

59

at, to let the abyss alone" [42]—and the Abyss! But the Mystery in which (or Whom) our life is held never leaves us completely to our own devices. No man but has

> felt through all this fleshly dresse
> Bright *shootes* of everlastingnesse.[43]

Events strike us, carrying "a light that never was, on sea or land." [44] You name them: a child's tears, Hitler's death in a fiery cellar, a certain chord in "The Fifth Symphony," the Sainte-Chapelle spiring above the Law Court, an astronaut confessing the wonders of successive sunrises, another astronaut claiming (as one belonging only to nature) "I am an eagle," [45] a wall between East and West Berlin. You name the event. Listen to other men as they name their event: "I remember that she was wearing a green dress," or, "I never really knew my sister until the day of our mother's funeral," or, "There in the laboratory it came on me like a flash," or, "The U-2 raises the whole question of espionage." Every event is miraculous, if by miracle we mean (as the Bible essentially means) that which brings sudden awareness of the vertical line. No man is bereft. Besides, he can expose himself to the Great Event.

What is the rightful word? Progress is a word half-blind, and forwardness (though it begs no questions) is not enough, for it carries no confession of the other dimension. Perhaps the answer is in some such word as "witness" or "sacrament." The word we have used is Dialogue—in the language of events. A Man is killed on a cross. Is that progress? Surely it was retrogression, for many forms of human pride conspired to kill him. But it could still be witness—to the Light that strikes on history; and it could still be sacrament, the evidence that life is not merely mundane, but "an outward and visible sign of an inward and invisible grace." [46] Grace is the characteristic New Testament word. It means the free gift of God to timebound and blundering men. The art of life and the interpretation of history may be this: so to live, since we cannot be spectators only, that our journey is cut by Light—Light awaited, longed-for, welcomed in whatever pain, and answered. It has been said of Michelangelo that he could take a hog-bristle brush, a few greasy pigments, and a stucco wall (could any items be more earthy?), and soon people saw God.[47] He bore witness. His act was sacramental. He made the right answers in the Dialogue. A student recently upbraided me for "the damned eschatology of the Church." He thought there should be only one dimension in life: the horizontal. He made a point, for the Church has sometimes believed that there is only the other dimension. But we live in two worlds. Any book, Bible or modern novel, that does not have the double stress, eschatological Mystery and accepted earthiness, is distortion. I have told elsewhere of seeing a desert town in which the only really green spot was the cemetery.[48] Was that progress, while fields still lacked irrigation? No, the desert rightly claims water. But the cemetery was still witness—to a World in which this little world is held.

V

Is the world getting better? The word "progress" offers no sufficient clue. It is on the earthline, and so begins and ends in earthiness, as modern history amply testifies. Besides, that line gives us no fixed points of measurement, for the road of history is "from everlasting to everlasting." [49] The Hebrew could mean, "from hidden time to hidden time," or, so far as history is concerned, "from the hiding place of time through time to the hiding place of time." What is implied by "getting better"? If we live also on a vertical line, if our days are always a crux, a point where two lines cross, then a Man on a cross may be the crux of history and the new measure of man's life "until we all attain to the unity of the faith and of the knowledge of the Son of God, to mature manhood, to the measure of the stature of the fullness of Christ." [50]

There is a further summing-up: we cannot ask the question as to the world's betterment as if we were merely spectators. For we are involved in history: shaped by it, but also shapers of it.

61

The question now becomes, "Am I getting better?" That is followed by another: "Better by what measure?" On one line of measurement, I am on the way to death. By the other? Paul Tillich has written that "history exists where there is decision, namely a decision which is concrete on the one hand, and which is rooted in the depths of the Unconditioned on the other hand." [51] If someone asks, "Is the world getting better?" the answer is, "What do you and I think, and what shall we do?" That is followed by, "In this once-for-all encounter of history, on what line shall we chiefly live?" Then comes a blurted prayer— man's answer in the Dialogue: to the Mystery in Whom alone life finds meaning:

O God, who art, and wast, and art to come, before whose face the generations rise and pass away, age after age the living seek thee and find that of thy faithfulness there is no end. Our fathers in their pilgrimage walked by thy guidance, and rested on thy compassion; still to their children be thou the cloud by day, and the fire by night. . . . Not of our worthiness, but of thy tender mercy hear our prayer; for the sake of Jesus Christ thy Son our Lord. Amen.[52]

CHAPTER IV

History as Paradox

HISTORY IS NOT A SIMPLE STORY. THE HISTORIAN'S TASK IS HARDLY begun when he writes, "This happened." In fact he cannot fully know what happened. His net of words cannot catch the sorrow of a feudal serf or Saint Joan's rapture in her martyrdom. Moreover, the light of any event must pass through the prism of his mind and culture, and so suffer refraction. There are no bare facts: they come clothed in interpretation, and each writing of history gives them new garb. That is to say, all past events carry faith and invite new faith. Only in faith can history be construed. What faith?

These chapters propose that faith in Christ is the clue to the meaning of history. The proposal is so alien from the mind of our generation as to seem "sheer indoctrination," the branding on history of the mark of a bigotry. Biblical thought, despite its daringness (or because of it), is not even studied nowadays, let alone understood. Its massive contours and quivering thrusts are a lost continent. Meanwhile the modern mind is blandly unaware that it has indoctrinations of its own, such as a naïve faith in "progress," or the belief that rational mind can spell out every mystery and proceed to fashion a rational world.

But faith in Christ as the revelatory focus of history is never an easy faith, and the alienation of our time is not its major foe. The main trouble is that history itself seems to contradict it; that, indeed, history seems to contradict any pattern which our minds propose. In short, history seems paradox or contradiction. If we say, "history repeats," we are confronted by undeniable newness as in our suddenly nuclear age. If we plead that man is too intelligent to wage war, a claim made by Comte [1] and the early humanists, two world wars deny us, with more cruelty per square mile and more square miles than even Dracula could dream. A paradox is not an untruth: by the meaning of the word it is that which goes against accepted opinion or "common sense." A paradox, despite our modern use of the word, is not necessarily a flat contradiction: the terms of its dilemma may be resolved in a higher term. If history always has a paradoxical cast, if it escapes every net thrown by any historian—Spengler, Toynbee, Sorokin, Plekhanov—as we shall try to show, we must ask why. Such is our present task. So we now turn to instances of the paradox.

I

Here is an instance: history seems both repetitive and unique. Men have long ago guessed that "history repeats." Perhaps Thucydides first used the phrase,[2] but it may have been a cliché of the man in the street before his time, as it is in our time. Who could deny its partial truth? Here is a tiny item: the veil which women now wear in an open car was high fashion in the first days of the automobile. Here is a large item: there is a cycle of birth, growth, decline, and death for cultures as for individual men. Maybe our eyes "give to history" this cyclic cast, and maybe we have borrowed the pattern from the cycles of nature, which cannot rightfully be printed on the vitalities of history. But surely there is evidence in history itself, or why should we say, "history repeats," and why should our neighbor nod his head? Then is history worse than a squirrel-cage, worse because it holds a man and not only a squirrel?

Chaos, Cosmos! Cosmos, Chaos! once again the sickening game;
Freedom, free to slay herself, and dying while they shout her name.[3]

Suppose planets and constellations and all orders of life are blind amoral recurrence.

We stay our journey to suggest that the proper word may be,

not recurrence, but typology. The early Church had no New Testament, and had no need, for it found in the Old Testament foreshadowings enough and to spare concerning Christ. Sometimes these prophesies were strained to the breaking point. Thus the word about Nazareth, "that it might be fulfilled which was spoken by the prophets, 'He shall be called a Nazarene'," [4] is not even grammatically correct, for the word in the Old Testament is not Nazarene but Nazorene, which means an ascetic or anchorite. But this looking back to find a type of experience is not therefore absurd, for who could doubt that Isaiah fifty-three, with its, "He was despised and rejected by men; a man of sorrows, and acquainted with grief;" [5] whatever its original reference, has found fulfillment in Christ? And who could deny that the groups around the Cross—ambitious ecclesiastics, reactionary Sadducees, too-virtuous Pharisees, violent Zealots, and Essenes seeking monastic escape—have their counterparts in our day? Perhaps history would be sheer bafflement if there were not these typologies. The question is a hot spot in modern Biblical inquiry. But it is not now our main concern.

For what we must now say is that, just when we have decided that history is recurrence, it confronts us with a startling newness. For history is a field of unique emergents. The saying that no man enters an old river is true, yet only half true; for not only is the stream new moment by moment, but the man also is new moment by moment. History is event-ful, and the events are not the monotone of a Buddhist drum. Sulphuric acid is not merely "composed of" two parts hydrogen, one part of sulphur, and four parts of oxygen: the acid is a new thing, with properties both destructive and healing which its components cannot claim. But sulphuric acid in this regard is no true parable of what happens in history with its ever-changing convergences, for the "elements" of human freedom are unpredictable in their "conspiracies," whereas the "conspiracies" of nature can partly be foreseen. Each man is unique, even to his fingerprint. Each moment of his life is unique. His give-and-take with other men and within himself—and under the Mystery—is unique moment

65

by moment. Our time is a new thing under the sun, for it moves towards one culture, nay, towards one technological culture, with nuclear powers. Mankind has not passed this way before. Early communism and early capitalism are both already obsolete. Even the temporal "good" or "gain" in ancient systems vanishes, "lest one good custom should corrupt the world." [6] History is a paradox of repetition and uniqueness. Arnold Toynbee can never fully compare civilizations, for each is new; and to draw analogies from ancient China for our own time is indeed a hazardous affair. [7]

Here is another paradox: history is both irrational and purposeful. R. G. Collingwood in his *The Idea of History* holds that history is concerned only with the act-ual, that is, with man's acts. He thus separates history from science, [8] and is centrally right, for history and nature are discrepant realms. Yet the two dimensions intersect: for man's body is of the dust of the ground. What if the natural stage collapses while the human action "takes place"? History is occasioned by the San Francisco earthquake. Thus the "fatalities" of nature (interesting word: fatealities) invade history; and nature sometimes seems irrational, at least to historical eyes. Why should a flash flood in the Pennsylvania hills sweep away an orphanage? To pretend that we would know if we knew more science is—pretense. We might know more about science, but would we know more about the crisscross of dimensions—why *those* children in *that* orphanage perished at *that* time? Meanwhile there are darker irrationalities in the secrecies of the historical order. When a criminal says, "I don't know why I killed her," he is not necessarily a liar, for when does any man know more than some of the "causes" of any action? The rash of juvenile delinquency in our time has certain fairly clear antecedents, but others are hidden—in the individual subconscious, in the racial unconscious, and in the unpredictable coming together of the "right" components. Hitler's Germany or the sudden blackout of an

66

engine driver cannot fully be "explained." There is an irrational streak in history.

Again we stay our journey to remark that no philosophy or explanation can "solve" the "problem of pain." Some interpretations only rub sand into the wound. "Pain is discipline," we say, and so it is; but in what sense is a tidal wave discipline for those who perish or for children made orphans? "Pain is to teach us sympathy," we say, and that may happen if the right faith is involved; but it is not clearly evident that two world wars have taught mankind to sympathize. "Pain is the sepia in the picture," we say, thus proposing that God is a devil, for only a devil could plan the destruction of Pompeii to throw the Island of Capri into bright relief. Nietzsche with his, "Only as an aesthetic phenomenon is existence and the world eternally justified," [9] was close to this blasphemy. Even when we say, "God does not send pain," which is what we should say, we must add that "He allows it." So the mystery remains, for we must then ask, "Why does He allow it?" The Augustinian antinomy then confronts us: if God is good, he is not God; if God is God, He is not good.[10] Pain itself is paradox: it is "solved" only from a term above pain —by an Event: the Cross is the convergence of both pain and culpability, and should be history's blackest stigma. But it is not! Why? Because if God "allows" pain, He can also transmute it! But back to our journey, and to the other term of a paradox.

Just when we say that history is irrational it reveals purpose. All science assumes purpose. Otherwise there could be no science. Hypothesis suggests experiment, and that yields clearer understanding, and that in turn proposes a better hypothesis. It is that kind of world. As with nature, so in part with the world of men. We can formulate languages and plan currencies; and, insofar as trade is honest, there will follow a certain stanch coherence in the body social. Our American doctrine of progress is not so much naïve as heretical: it claims for man what belongs only to God. But the heresy could not have risen except as deviation from a true surmise, namely, that history has a purpose—so that man is able to ask, "What is the meaning of history?" How

67

strange that amid all the fatefulness of human freedom, politics is still a valid quest! How strange that history is not a raveled chaos, but a tapestry of which we ask, "What does this portray?" Good statesmanship is the right reading of events and the proposal of realistic action: it assumes that history will honor, at least in measure, our honorable purpose—because history itself is purpose. Jesus seems to have assured men of this trustworthiness in our human story: "You know how to interpret the appearance of the sky, but you cannot interpret the signs of the times." [11] Here he compares the dependability of nature with the sure purposes of history. So each man says of public and private pilgrimage: "There's a divinity that shapes our ends." [12] Yet how can purpose be irrational, and irrationality show purpose?

So to another paradox: history is both progress and retrogression. The two sometimes synthesize in frustration. Are they only the ebb and flow of the tides? We have suggested that the word "progress" should be challenged. Yet so many people have made friends with it that it cannot be altogether empty or treacherous. There is progress in knowledge: we know more than our fathers about astronomy and physics. There is progress in the amenities of life: men tending oil burners in a modern ocean liner are better off than their predecessors sweating before coal furnaces. Similarly transportation has canceled the physical estrangement between men and nations. Women are no longer the chattel possession of men: the home has become a partnership. These boons raise questions, such as, "Are they on the horizontal line or on the vertical?" [13] and, "Can we trust a world in which all men die for the sake of a Godlike posterity—which never arrives?" Immanuel Kant flirted with that latter question, as when he wrote that "it is always a subject of wonder that the older generations appear only to pursue their weary toil for the sake of those who come after them, . . . and that it is to be the happy fate of only the latest generations to dwell in the building upon which the long series of their forefathers have

68

labored, without so much as intending it and yet with no possibility of participating in the happiness which they were preparing." [14] But there is progress of a kind.

But now the other side of the paradox: "the building" to which Kant confidently looked has been broken in two world wars, and the misuse of nuclear power may destroy it. Perhaps progress is a "gold brick." Cartoons such as "The Flintstones," [15] which show ancient man engaged in our modern follies, come from the half-notion that modern man is primitive: only his clothes are up-to-date. The bloodletting of our wars, the decline of work-morality, the prevalence of bribery in both politics and business, not to mention the cheap thrills which pass for pleasure, are no warrant for Horatio Alger [16] pride. Is Dachau [17] to be reckoned "progress"? The word forgets the fatefulness of man's freedom. "Progress" in technology may become the means of mass murder. The new automation may be Frankenstein. The new physics may incinerate the planet. The new home may dwindle into a cult of new houses. The new leisure may be laziness, and the new conquest of venereal disease may lead to license. A city is now concerned for one lost child, yet we bomb cities and kill thousands of children. So what price progress? If we look at history on a horizontal line we see only ebb and flow. Arnold Toynbee has told us that his study of history began when he pondered the drama of Faust and Mephistopheles.[18] Why did he then sidetrack that story, and propose instead a mammoth rubber stamp for civilizations? The controversy in heaven, whatever its mystery, a vast warfare between love and demonism, may be a better clue. Progress and retrogression are in paradox.

Here is a still stranger paradox: man feels himself responsible in history, yet history sometimes shows scant concern for his dutiful endeavors. Thus a paradox of requirement and wantonness. We assume human freedom, and have little option; for if we deny freedom, we assume that the denial is free, not merely the lip movements of a marionette. Similarly we assume that freedom is responsible freedom, as when we say, "he was brave" or "he was a coward." If we confess, as we must, that we have small right to judge our neighbors since we cannot read their inner history and may be ignorant even of their outward circumstance, and since we also have a tarnished record, we thus make a larger confession, namely, that we are all under a higher court. Our duty is not merely towards "posterity," for "posterity" is not God. If we insist on defining our obligation as "social concern," there is always at the back of our mind remembrance of the fact that both we and our neighbors are created, and that certain "values" (sainted word) inhere in human life which must be honored. When Ralph Tyler Flewelling writes: "Democracy possesses no power to give insight or honesty," and then discusses "a blind trust in the efficacy of Democracy spelled with a capital D," [19] he is telling us that our responsibility goes beyond men, even though he does not rigorously pursue his own insight.

Yet history seems often to scorn the responsible man, nay to throw him on history's rubbish-heap as if he were only broken clay.

> The best-laid schemes o' mice an' men
> Gang aft agley [20]

as if men were no more important than mice.

> Now and again to some lone soul or other
> God speaks, and there is hanging to be done.[21]

But why should the God-chosen man be hung? Why is the responsible individual made victim of the blind crowd? Israel could never understand why she was scourged by Assyria. She admitted that judgment had rightly fallen, or so at least her prophets knew; but Assyria!—Assyria was blind to God and His judgments, and worshiped only idols! So we ask why a megalomaniac paperhanger should bedevil the world. Yes, the seeds of

70

Hitlerism were in every land, but the world arraigned against him was not Hitler. Bright eras come, not by man's contriving; dark eras, not by man's intention and desire. We are still responsible, but history ever and again appears irresponsible, as if there were no right and wrong.

We are proposing that whatever pattern we offer as the explanation of history there are facts which falsify and contradict us. One final instance, among many that still confront us, is the Marxist claim. What a neat pattern! And how its simplicity beguiles simple and rebellious minds! Mark its outlines. First everything comes from matter, so mind comes from matter; and therefore mind, though we should not deny its freedom, is free only in its sole area, which is matter: materialism is the only possible philosophy. (Notice our old friend "came from":[22] no room for unpredictable newness in the course of creation; and notice the worship of the time sequence: what comes before is better, so by strict application the ape man is better than Lenin!) Next: as to history, there is a dialectic, claim and counter-claim, so that class ownership of tools must be followed by mass ownership. The flow of human story is thesis, antithesis, and synthesis. The synthesis, following the class thesis and the mass antithesis, is the Soviet Republic. (Notice the outright borrowing of the Hegelian dialectic, which was proposed for the study of philosophy, and is not a profound reading even in that field. Notice also the stubborn refusal to ask of the alleged synthesis, "What next?" If we pursue the fantastic logic, the Soviet Republic must now become the new thesis, for no man can petrify history.) Next: combine the above two premises, and it follows that history is determined by matter in the field of economic force. All that men do and say is so controlled. Religion, to cite but one item, is not real: it is a smoke screen sent up by the classes, who temporarily have the cash and the tools, to try to stay the inevitable movement of the dialectic: it is an anodyne to keep the poor in deception and submission. This

71

logic is so patently childish that it could never have gained headway except for a rightful mass indignation.

Georgi Plekhanov's famous essay on "The Role of the Individual in History" [23] is already a classic statement. Lenin described him as the brains of "The Revolution," and together they wrote the "Party" program of 1903. The essay tells us that there are no great men (it conducts heroes to the rim of the void and gives them the toe), for great men are the product of economic forces. (It never occurred to Plekhanov that his essay therefore was but another regurgitation from the economic gullet.) The essay informs us also that the fatalism of the dialectic need not choke Russian enthusiasm, for look at the Calvinists: they believed in election and were yet tireless in their zeal. Plekhanov forgot that the word enthusiasm is *en theos*, in God, and that it comes precisely because men believe in human responsibility, not in a cast-iron world and human robots; and he was ignorant of the range, balance, and depth of the Biblical doctrine of election. The essay then proceeds to show how every historical episode runs back in a direct line to the economic matrix. One main instance chosen, not with tongue in cheek but with stolid soberness (communism can have no sense of humor, for humor can hardly come from hammer and sickle), is, believe it or not, the liaison between Louis XV and Madame Pompadour! Read it: the essay at that point is unwittingly funnier than *The New Yorker*.

Before we mark how this pattern has been falsified, we should confess its measure of truth. It could hardly have gathered such a head of steam if there were no fire in its "innards." No historian can write now without some awareness of the "Revolution." Man is whole man: his mind shapes his work, but what he does with his hands during the days in the week shapes his mind. He is psyche-soma, a psychosomatic unity, not a "spiritual soul" in an unfortunate body. The body also is of the essence of personhood. Any religion blind to these facts is not pertinent, but impertinent. Industrialism is a mighty force as Plekhanov believed; yes, in ways he never guessed, for our machines may

72

now mechanize us, conditioning us to an automatic response; and thus make us vulnerable to just such tyrannies as that which has fastened on Russia.

But our question is this: does the Marxist pattern explain history? There could hardly be a more obvious "no." The contradictory facts are already written in history. The "workers of the world" did not unite around the Marxist coup. Forces other than economic were busily engaged, such as home, sex (Louis XV and Madame Pompadour!), sports, culture, nation, and a great barrier known as language; and, in addition, spires pointing to the mysterious sky. Of these forces which is strongest? Which is most enduring? It is certain that they cannot all be dismissed in favor of a hand holding a hammer, for life refuses to gather to a childish simplification. Meanwhile capitalism under democracy proved flexible enough to grant leeway to labor unions and social legislation. Meanwhile the monolithic structure of Marxism began to crack. The new leaders cannot remember the days of actual revolution or the peonage from which it sprang. The Soviet found need for purges within "the party"; liquidation of the bourgeois leaders was not enough. Why? Because the Russian definition of sin, ownership of tools and private property, is not enough! Sin is the egocentric pride of the creature which often flaunts property, but which has many another form, such as administrative control, public adulation, even vodka and caviar, and above all political power. Meanwhile every time Khrushchev accuses his enemies of bad faith he introduces norms far deeper than the play of economic force.

II

But no more "patterns." We have cited five, to show that history always eludes the neat "explanation." We could continue the list. History is *both true and false*, for instance; for do we not say that "we must await the verdict of history" while agreeing at the same time with Robert Walpole, "Do not read history, for that I know must be false." [24] You continue the list:

73

history is *both determined and free*: determined, because historians, not to mention psychologists and cultural anthropologists, can always trace causal antecedents (as witness William L. Shirer's fine account of Hitler's Germany),[25] and can do it confidently if they blink the mystery in the word "cause"; while other men will point both to human responsibility and to *kairoi*, strange gatherings of factors (sometimes apocalyptic and explosive in their force) on which history pivots to a new turn. History is *both social and individual*. But enough: history is paradox or contradiction. No historian can split the terms of a paradox. An ideology is a feckless sham. Now we ask, Why this paradox? Obviously there can be no full answer: only hints and gleams as we confront paradox within mystery. But we may be aware of meanings, even if explanations are always confounded. So we offer the following, not for "learning," but for some slim guidance "for us men and for our salvation" [26] as we are responsibly involved in history.

History comes as paradox because our eyes and nature are paradox. We are not merely flesh, or we could not use words such as "good" and "bad"; but we are not disembodied spirits, or we would not have to eat, sleep, and die. We are not in the natural order alone, for we speak to ourselves at first sight of the Ginza, "How strange that you, my self, should be walking down the main street of Tokyo!" But we are not altogether supernatural, for our feet are on the sidewalk, and even if we were an astronaut, our tiny capsule would have to simulate earth conditions. We are "above" the historical order, and yet involved in it. So we view history both from the inside and the outside; and, unlike physicists studying light, we can find no "principle of complementarity"; [27] for we are dealing, not with the fairly predictable world of nature, but with the fatefulness of man's freedom and with the mystery of history's origin and destiny. Karl Mannheim, admitting the subjective element in any study of history, suggests that we can combine the various

74

perspectives of one man or many men, and so reach a common denominator.[28] Intelligent men can be naïve!

If man lives a two-dimensional life, if his very mind is amphibian, and if the horizontal line of his pilgrimage is cut by the vertical, it is not strange that he can find no neat pattern in history's fabric. Arnold Toynbee's erudite *Study* [29] shifts backwards and forwards between his proffered pattern (with its astonishing detail, consistently for each civilization: initiative, time of trouble, decline, rise of religion, rally, and rout)—between that on the one hand, and on the other a reference to a dialogue in heaven between God and the Devil! H. A. L. Fisher found no plan:

Men wiser and more learned than I have discerned in history a plot, a rhythm, a predetermined pattern. These harmonies are concealed from me. I can see only one emergency following upon another as wave follows upon wave, only one great fact with respect to which, since it is unique, there can be no generalizations.[30]

Remarkably many modern historians quote this passage—E. H. Carr, Arnold Toynbee, Charles Frankel, Reinhold Niebuhr; Dr. Carr dismisses it as a "banal remark," [31] while others view it with this or that measure of sympathetic understanding. Pieter Geyl, in his debate with Arnold Toynbee, confesses "the infinite complexity . . . of phenomena and incidents" in history and "their shadowy and changing nature," [32] but does not mention the complexity of each historian. How can paradoxical man find a neat explanation for paradoxical history?

We try and always fail. Geyl again: "The attempt to reduce them [historical facts] . . . to a scheme of absolute validity can never lead to anything but disappointment." [33] Thus Jules Jusserand, shortly before his death, in a radio broadcast from France as a farewell to America, said: "Remember this also, and be well persuaded of its truth: the future is not in the hands of Fate, but in ours." [34] Would he be so confident today? Is history ever in human hands? They fall and die. But, we should

75

add, there may be meaning even where there can be no explanation. A paradox is resolved only as its terms are gathered into a higher term. Is the paradox of human nature resolved in "the Word was made flesh"? [35] That is Biblical faith. And the paradoxes of history? The Bible says boldly, "In Him all things cohere." [36] But he also is paradox, Victor-Victim coming to his throne by way of a gallows!

Again: history appears as paradox because our sight is sinfully impaired. History itself is raveled by our guilty blundering. The word sin is not easily accepted in our time, partly because it is confused with psychotic guilt, partly because Mrs. Grundy [37] has tried to claim it, and partly because it brings everyone under judgment. No man can write about it without himself being indicted. But the word stands—for the egocentricity of the creature. We are not content to walk the narrow road between the natural order and the other order from which already we can view life. We sink into the lower world, all the way from local "status" to Hitler's "blood and soil"; [38] or we pretend we belong only to the higher world, and try to play God. Our job during mortal years is to witness to heaven in the midst of earth, but we refuse that assignment, though it is large enough even to the point of rapture and pain. So history is bedeviled. How can we then expect to find any neat, clean plan?

Meanwhile our inward life also is raveled. Our eyes, too literally, are bloodshot. Said Jesus: "If your eye is sound, your whole body will be full of light; but if your eye is not sound, your whole body [including the mind addressed to the problem of history] "will be full of darkness. If then the light in you is darkness, how great is the darkness!" [39] So great that we can find no clue to the pageant of man's life on earth! One moment our word is "progress," and the next it is "failure." But is not this the manic mark: a burst of confidence followed by a trough of depression? Now we confess our obligation, and now allege that history gives us no chance. But is not this the way of all guilty men: to be alternately contrite and self-justifying? Spiritual things are "spiritually discerned": [40] it is always partly true that we see what we are. History seems ambiguous because our life is culpably ambiguous. So history is the history of redemption. History is sick, a truant child crying in the night, and only Love and Power from beyond our timebound world can save us. The Christian claim makes little sense to merely academic minds, but "comes alive" to men who know their eyes are bloodshot: "Who for us men and for our salvation came down . . . and was made man." [41]

But the major reason why history seems ambiguous is this: it is not our kingdom to order and control. It is under another Sovereignty. Yes, we bedevil the proud pageant of man's pilgrimage. We turn it into what Toynbee calls "rally and rout." [42] But there are limits set to our control, or history might long ago have ended; and there are bounds which evil cannot pass, for at long last the Devil is a fool. The origin and destiny of man's story are both Mystery, and his journey is always beset by Mystery: "from Whom we come, to Whom we go." [43] The strange turns and junctures are not ours to determine, even though we do have our small partnership. A measure of evil comes unaccountably from our projected good, for a man cannot even join a church without appearing to draw a self-righteous line between himself and his neighbors; and good springs from our projected evil, so that the Cross of Christ breaks into light. Meanwhile our calculated risks bring incalculable threat. We cannot know the "times or seasons": [44] the Greek words mean respectively the duration of dynasties and the crucial turns of event: they are set in God's authority. It is not our world. Yet, and therefore, it keeps integrity, so that historians inquire as to its meaning.

Man the creature cannot construe the ways of God the Creator. That is why we cannot "explain" history. If we saw Him, we would be "blinded" by "excess of light." [45] If we understood, we would ourselves be incredible God. "One great emergency following upon another," wrote H. A. L. Fisher, "as

77

wave follows upon wave"; and E. H. Carr with unimpressive mind dismisses the sentence as a "banal remark." [46] History is an island, with wave after wave breaking on the shore; and we are children walking on the beach, trying to find the ocean's secret. "Deep calls to deep," [47] the Mystery of birth to the Mystery of death, across our narrow spit of land. We listen to the whispers and thunders of the inviolate sea, for we know, dimly or poignantly, that the meaning of our life is not on shore. How can we expect to know the plan of history, much less to impose it? An ideology is the final conceit. We can know God only as He tells us. The Bible word is "revelation." Little ships keep coming in from the beyond; and one day long ago, but as recently as today, "a Ship sailed into Bethlehem." [48] Maybe that is how we find meaning (not an "explanation"), because meaning finds us.

So, as upshot, history is paradox because it is meant to be a field for faith. History does not answer to the curious mind, but only to the total adventure of the total man. We are agents, not merely spectators. Faith is not make-believe, but basic trust, not unlike the trust which a scientist gives to his world; yet wider (all comprehensive) and deeper (to the uttermost depth) and involving the whole man. Faith is not circular reasoning, but the sword which cuts reason's endless circles. It is man's response in his total self to the onset of the Mystery in the event of Christ. An aviator, knowing that his small plane was about to crash, deliberately avoided a playground and a busy street where he might have landed with some chance of survival, and made for a sandpit where it was almost certain he would be killed. To reason about such an event would be a circle indeed, for there is no neat answer to such questions as why men love danger, or why such a man should die when he is needed in public life, or why mechanisms and mechanics fail. The event seizes us, and faith is our response.

How does faith confront paradox? It accepts it in its tension and pain. It gathers it into a higher term, which is the only way in which paradox can ever be solved. It is paradox that our human nature is both individual and social; therefore the "answer" is above both "horns" of the seeming contradiction. Individual right and the corporate bond can be held in unity only as both are obedient to a higher will. Does history seem both circle and new thrust? The circle is for faith's guidance as faith looks to the past, and the new thrust is for zest. Is history both purpose and "fate"? The purpose enlists faith as witness, and the "fate" is reminder that God is an abyss of Mystery. Is history both progress and tragic failure? The failure drives faith to God by way of the "failure" of the Cross, while the progress is the gift of grace. Is history both obligation and wantonness? Faith says of the obligation, "Lo, I have come to do thy will"; [49] and of the seeming wantonness, just what Lincoln said in a dark hour: "The judgments of the Lord are true and righteous altogether." [50] Pascal has told us that the heart has its reasons, which reason does not know.[51] Faith in action has eyes when our natural eyes cannot see.

III

If history has any pattern, it is the patternless pattern of the dialogues within each man's life—under the Dialogue, the successive configurations through which he tries to realize himself. He talks to himself about this and that. Not only the theme constantly changes, but the two men within himself. Now the policeman speaks with the man tempted to thieve: "I wouldn't do it, if I were you. It breaks society, and there is a jail for thieves." Now the statesman listens to the voter: "I know I should vote for So-and-so, but it might be bad for business, and, besides, I have always prided myself on the straight party line." The inner dialogues are beyond plan or computation. Meanwhile the man talks to his neighbors, not only in private conversation, but in the endless configurations of social concern. Meanwhile a Voice keeps breaking in on all the conversations: "Who are you? Why are you?" "Where were you when I laid the foundation of the earth?" [52] We cannot bring such a life to a neat plan.

Yet it is a unity, for the person is a person in the wholeness and continuity of experience, and history itself is a "unique fact," [53] and God is God. The keys of both person and history are hung behind God's door.

So we are back with the faith that Christ is the redemption of history. He gives it focus, brings it under judgment, and grants it grace. He entered into history's paradox, and found it as taut as the Cross. "The Word became flesh," [54] a piece of history, "and tented among us." The dwelling of the Holy was pitched among the black, huddled tents of men. The heaven was not empty when He came. The Mystery was not resolved. But the Mystery was disclosed. The strange paradoxes of our human story were gathered into the saving paradox of His life and death. The Victor-Victim entered by shame into His glory. The Dialogue repeats and is new; clear as to our obligation, but ever and again hidden in Mystery; progressing as man listens, sinking as he disobeys; social as God speaks to the group, but always the secret of the secret heart. But the consistency abides beyond any pattern, because God is God—in Jesus Christ.

IV

The Matthew Arnold sonnet tells of a preacher going his rounds in a squalid London slum. He spoke zestfully to one who asked him how he fared:

> I of late have been
> Much cheered with thoughts of Christ, *The living bread.*

Arnold himself, despite his skepticism, underlined the last three words, and then made his comment:

> O human soul! as long as thou canst so
> Set up a mark of everlasting light,
> Above the howling senses' ebb and flow.[55]

But the preacher did not set up the mark. God set it up, the mark of a Cross, for surely men never intended its saving power.

It stands not only above "the howling senses' ebb and flow," but above the stranger tides of our human story. If we keep it in sight we shall be "much cheered," even when history becomes a slum —or a calcined wilderness, for we shall then look to the fulfillment of history, when we shall know as we are known.

CHAPTER V

History, Necessity, and Freedom

OUR TIME IN HISTORY FEARS IT IS DETERMINED: IN SHORT, THAT it has no freedom. We study psychology, and then wonder if there is any escape from psychological antecedent leading on to psychological consequent, the subconscious being devil in the drama, the drama being no drama, but only link after link in an unbreakable chain. The links are not only within each man's psyche, but they are from parent to child back to the beginning of history. It is strange indeed that a typical Freudian should first profess shock at any doctrine of original sin, and then propose the doctrine in new form and in such darkness as Calvinism at its worst never proposed or even dreamed. We study biology, and end in the same fear: we are victims of "natural law" in our bodies and in our iron world. Then we turn to sociology, with the same drear result: a child born in the slums of Chicago, Irish or Italian or Negro as one national or racial group follows another (it does not matter which group), has little chance: culture and mores caught in poverty and deprivation brand him for life.

This mood, which is in many instances not mood only but conclusion, afflicts the study of history more than other studies because history is the encompassing field. Our psychologies and sociologies are held in history. Even science is so caught and held, for the scientist, though primarily concerned with the natural order, is himself prisoner or agent in history. Historical necessity is the all-embracing bondage, unless we concede that dubious honor to the Devil. Is it not incredible that our minds, setting out in assumption of their real freedom, should now con-

82

clude that they are not free? Incredible, not comic or tragic, for in an iron world there is neither comedy nor tragedy; incredible, for the conclusion reached means that mind is not mind, but only meaninglessness or nonsensical motion. Literally incredible: not possible of being believed! If we went to the garage and heard our automobile say, "I am only a car," we would know it is a liar; and a liar cannot be "only a car." We would look for the hidden man. Perhaps the proper question nowadays is not, "Are we free?" but, "Why are we in flight from freedom?"

I

It should not surprise us that there are roughly three types of historical theory. One of them is determinist. The instance might be the writings of Henry Thomas Buckle.[1] Two gross misunderstandings, he tells us, have hindered the study of history: the dogmas respectively of free will and predestination. History is a science. It has no place for free will, which is a figment of "consciousness" without "proof"; or for predestination, a theological imposition which by its very nature is beyond our human ken. We must learn to study history as the scientist studies nature, combining the disciplines of economist, lawyer, meteorologist, physicist, geographer, and above all statistician. (Who is to be this angel-intellect he does not tell us.) We would have understood history before now if historical phenomena had not been a little more complex than the data of the separate sciences, and if historians had not been of "inferior ability." If we proceed scientifically we shall know without doubt that "suicide is merely the product of the general condition of society" (notice the "merely": scientism has no compassions), "and that the individual felon only carries into effect the necessary consequences of preceding circumstances." We gasp, or should gasp. But this nonsense is not dead in our time, and we have less excuse, for we do not live in the first flush of "the advance of science," and we know of two world wars. By Buckle's own argument, his writing also is "merely the

83

product" of society's condition, like suicide (very like it), and he himself is only a "necessary consequent" like felony! Spengler forgot that his *The Decline of the West* is by his own theory only another instance of inevitable decay.[2] Plekhanov would have been angry had somebody told him that his famous or infamous essay [3] is but another vomiting of the economic vortex. All three men argue and urge. But why, when nobody has any choice?

There are meliorist views, aware of the self-contradiction which always falsifies determinism, yet not quite ready to accept the fatefulness of freedom. Tolstoy's approach is a curious instance. He admits freedom, but pleads that it cannot be a factor in historical study, for "if each man could act as he pleased, all history would be a series of disconnected incidents." [4] He does not stop to ask if freedom could ever mean doing as we please. No, intent on "laws for the whole of humanity," he proposes the following parallel: just as we find truth in astronomy by abandoning the notion of a static planet, so we find truth in history by "renouncing the direct feeling of the independence of one's own personality." Again we gasp, or should gasp. But this nonsense also is still with us. Tolstoy, like Buckle, is pretending that the scientist is not a scientist, but a camera computer; and that men are only objects, and that the historical order is but another instance of the natural order. The only answer is flat denial. Whatever may be said of the minor physical status of the planet Earth, people are not merely physical; and each man *does* have "independence of his own personality." The scientist himself assumes independence whenever he views nature. It is too bad Tolstoy discussed historical theory: his *Anna Karenina* [5] searches us to the depths, for in that book he rightly took for granted what his theory of history tries to deny.

John Stuart Mill is another curious advocate of the meliorist view. Much impressed by Buckle, and, like Buckle, under the spell of Auguste Comte, he was honest enough to admit the axiom of man's freedom. But he also was resolved to turn history

84

into science: it is a movement of "progress" guided by "an ad-vance in knowledge." [6] So individual freedom, he argues, is a minor vagary, and the vagaries offset one another; and therefore the new science, prosecuted with scientific vigor, can find the overarching law, with statistical study as main instrument. Thus "the very events" of freedom "which in their own nature appear most capricious and uncertain" (there he glimpsed the unpre-dictable in man's liberty) "when considerable numbers are taken into account" will yield "a degree of regularity approach-ing the mathematical." His instance, quoting Buckle,[7] is people who mail a letter unaddressed. Overall statistics can bring under control this "trifling and as it might appear accidental oc-curence." Notice the "as it might appear": man's scientific mind shall soon understand every variable in history! We gasp, or should gasp. But this nonsense also continues: a college student recently told me that man's intellect, though it may not know all that can be known about history, shall soon bring history under prediction control by means of "probability." If forget-fulness is "trifling," even the forgetting to address a letter, is a question. The destiny of empire might turn on it. Forgetfulness is not quantitative, but qualitative; not in the natural order, but in the historical order; and forgetfulness may raise a hurricane, as when a man forgets his wife's birthday; and forgetting God may bring world desolation. Arnold Toynbee is meliorist after his own fashion. His cycles are determinist, but his concession that our civilization has an open end of freedom is voluntarist [8] —though why ours should be open when all the others have obeyed his intricate pattern is not clear. So he straddles, and the midpoint of the straddle is meliorism. Then he ships in more confusion by his frequent quoting of Goethe's *Faust* as if he half believes that the secret of history is in heaven. Maybe it is!

The third view outrightly posits freedom as a vital factor in historical study: it is voluntarist. Isaiah Berlin, for instance, notes that no determinist ever escapes judgments of praise or blame, especially, we might add, in political debate. Then this, with

85

saving common sense: "If determinism were a valid theory of human behavior, these distinctions would be as inappropriate as the attribution of moral responsibility to the planetary system or the tissues of a living cell." [9] Austin Farrar cites as typical of our assumption of freedom the choice of a man driving a car. The man weighs alternatives: "Can I pass before that oncoming car reaches me? No, it would be wisdom to wait. Better safe than sorry!" Says Farrar: [10] if that choice is determined, by some psychological fear stemming from a childhood trauma, and by biological urges, and by an infantile awe of one's parents, and even by geography and climate—all these factors instantly becoming one so that they move the driver as he moves the brake— there is a constitutional perifidy in all creation, for to quote again from Berlin, "If the belief in freedom . . . is a necessary illusion, it is so deep and so pervasive that it is not felt as such." [11] No, life is impossible if history is by nature total deceitfulness. But there is a pit across the path of the voluntarist; he easily forgets the factor of necessity. Thus Carl Michaelson in words all too-sweeping: "Man is his freedom . . . He is not a nature with attributes. He is history." [12] He quotes Karl Jaspers with approval: "Freedom is where a series is begun out of nothing." [13] These quotations are too-hasty blast-offs into the void. Man is not God. Even a space capsule must simulate earth conditions. God works ex nihilo, even though that doctrine is from our finitude in necessary avowal and mystery, but man is creature, always under creaturely necessity.

II

What, then, is the relation of freedom and necessity? Of this debate, which any man enters with trepidation, we may say perhaps more than of any other:

> Myself when young did eagerly frequent
> Doctor and saint, and heard great argument
> About it and about: but evermore
> Came out by the same door where in I went.[14]

But this is clear: freedom and necessity cannot be separated: they are two sides of one shield. We say, "This is a world of natural law," thus trying to isolate necessity. But man is a psychosomatic unity, and he cannot remove that hyphen. In him necessity and freedom are subtly and inextricably interfused. The same verity holds of man's involvement in history. Certain statements follow.

There is no absolute freedom. None of us is "free as a bird." Only a bird is free as a bird; and a bird cannot swim like a tuna or walk like a man, but must live within its constitution. Similarly a fish leaping from the ocean onto the beach is not "free in a larger world," but simply dead. Epictetus said wisely, "If I were a swan, I would act like a swan." [15] Of course if he had been a swan he would have *had* to act like a swan, whereas a man in strange freedom may act like a "wolf," yet not with impunity. No man can pitch a tent on the sun, or grow lollipops on cactus plants, or give way to sadism and still be welcome at children's parties, or fly to the fabled isles by using the breast-stroke. He is within the necessities of his nature. Likewise he is in historical necessity. He lives in present history, not in the Middle Ages, and must so act. He is constrained by his land and its language, its culture, its "style," and its record in the total story of mankind. There are "structures" in history: a man is not determined by them, but he is "conditioned": they delineate his area of liberty. If he lives in the Western world he is subject to taxes from two world wars. If he lives in Mississippi his freedom of expression in favor of racial integration is not a wide sky. Meanwhile he must confront transience and death. No freedom is possible "outside the constitution"—his constitution and the structures of nature and history.

But there is no absolute necessity. If there were, we could not even breathe, except as an iron lung; and if we were iron lungs, we could not differentiate between iron lungs and human lungs. If necessity were absolute there could be no change, or at least no ability to mark change. Only a stance above time enables us to say, "Time is swift." Thus to speak is to point to an axiom

87

of consciousness, the very consciousness which Buckle tried to dismiss as lacking "proof," [16] the very consciousness in which he inescapably wrote the words! The dilemma of the determinist becomes comedy. Once I heard John B. Watson, the outright behaviorist, explain to a public meeting his proposal that even our passing thought is response to external stimulus, and then urge his listeners to propagate that truth as against a merely imagined voluntarism. When I asked how they could, since propagation and opposition, behaviorism and idealism, are all mere electric response to some external switch, he became flushed and angry. He refused to believe that his doctrine also is inevitable answer to a pressed button. Still less did he ask how all the buttons press themselves to make a world so self-consistent that it becomes a uni-verse. The determinist scolds his children, but why? One lately told me that both North and South are so "controlled" psychologically that they have no choice in the fierce debate about segregation; and then said: "I wonder what would have happened if Lincoln had chosen his original plan of compensation for the slave owners instead of civil war." Henry Thomas Buckle was sure that history under study would reveal a "uniformity with which, under the same circumstances, the same events must succeed each other";[17] but, of course, circumstances are never the same, and Mr. Buckle chose to write his book—instead of choosing some other form of drunkenness. No man escapes limitation; no man escapes the mystery of choice.

We can partly see what happens when we deny freedom. We ask, "Is the will free?" Then we say, "I must examine the will." Thus saying, we make the will an object. We set it "over there" to examine it. But an object is by nature not free: it is an object, and that is why all debates about free will are likely to end in a deterministic conclusion. Meanwhile the will is also "in here." It does the examining. It is free even to examine its own life! Thus we confront again the paradox of our human nature: we can view our own life. Self-transcendence is the locus of our freedom. Buckle in the quotation given above [18] dismisses "consciousness" as being "without proof," but uses consciousness (what else?) to write his denial of consciousness. He is pretending to be an electric eye. The examined will is not free; the examining will takes freedom for granted. Why we deny freedom is a fascinating question. Is it because in pride of mind we covet a neat understandable world? Is it because we make a mess of life, and then yearn for servitude that need not make decisions, saying with the prodigal in his mess, "Treat me as one of your hired servants"? [19] Is it because we dimly or secretly know that history is Dialogue, and try to escape the awestruck redeeming conversation?

We can partly see also the close relation between necessity and freedom. Suppose we are in a room with four doors and four windows, the room being on the twentieth floor of a skyscraper. We can make an exit by any of four doors. We can dive through one of the windows, but that is not recommended. But we cannot walk through the walls, or instantly sink through the floor, or fly through the ceiling. Ceiling, walls, and floor are destiny; the choice of doors is freedom. If there were no destiny in that room, there would be no choice of doors; indeed there would be no room. So freedom without destiny is a vacuum, and destiny without freedom is a steel block. Our endless debates set at opposites factors which are actually partners. Am I free or destined? The only possible answer is, "Both." This is the answer to the determinist and the voluntarist in history. As for the meliorist, he tries to find a midpoint when he should use a bracket.

What of history? It is a room, with destiny that thwarts us and with a choice of doors. Two world wars destine our present history—to taxes, for instance, to the despair that follows violence, to the self-blame which seeks relief in blaming other people. But we still have choice. We can be penitent or obdurate or censorious. We can vote for violence, on the one hand, which would smash what it cannot control (like Xerxes thrashing the flooded river with chains because it blocked his path),[20] or, on the other hand, we can commit ourselves to a patient way which seeks understanding, and builds bridges across

89

a gulf. Even the past is not a steel block, for it is always a carrier of both good and evil. We can choose from the past—Benedict Arnold or Abraham Lincoln. Nazism is past. Or is it? We curse communism, and almost praise the new Nazism, thus yielding to the monied pressure of men who reckon it revolutionary to say that two and two make four. Hitler's Nazism is historically past, yet it is not historical determinism: we can renounce it (the Bible word is penitence), or newly cleave to it. Does someone say that necessity sometimes breaks men—the helpless prisoners at Buchenwald? [21] That is tragedy, which we must discuss.[22] But the Bonhoeffer letters [23] show that even that door was not utterly blocked.

III

History is thus the struggle for freedom from outward fetters which men forge to bind their fellowmen. Basic necessity cannot be broken: space, time, responsibility, mortality, and certain historical structures. But there are human coercions, cultural mores, and political tyrannies which treat people as objects rather than as subjects, and which therefore should be broken. These are not "destiny," but an affront to destiny. So history has a recurrent theme:

> Go down Moses,
> 'Way down in Egypt land,
> Tell ole Pharaoh
> To let my people go! [24]

Note that "my": God is on the side of this revolt. The Magna Carta is a milestone. So is the Declaration of Independence. So is Lincoln's Second Inaugural. So is the rise of labor unions. Any of these deliverances may be perverted: labor union leaders may become corrupt. But when factories become tyrannous, with owners exercising control over people called "hands," it was right that the hands should join in protest, yes, even with the strike weapon when all other means were denied. This struggle for freedom may not be history's deepest motif, but it is a recurrent and rightful theme.

History is also the struggle of men to break the inner bond. But how? This fetter is self-forged by the misuse of freedom. Suppose a man sinks into things, or echoes the mass-mind, or becomes "yes-man" to a labor boss, or sells out in acquiescence to some vast commercial enterprise and so becomes "the organization man," what shall he do? The fetter is now in the man: how can a fetter break itself? Or a cripple turn handsprings in the back garden? To the Bible the inner fetter is a worse threat than the outer limitation, if only because it is closer to the vital springs of life. The existentialists call this inner surrender "an unauthentic life." [25] If "unauthentic" is a better word than "sinful," who knows? Sin is the inordinate self-concern of the creature, the pretense that he can be his own god, the pride in which perforce he becomes capsuled in himself. This is the real slavery: "Truly, truly, I say to you, every one who commits sin is a slave to sin." [26] Nay, the Bible goes further: when a man is inwardly free, he can endure or override the outer domination. Our time, its eyes set on "political freedom," can hardly understand this strange emphasis. We begin to understand, for our psychiatry is intent to break the inner chain. It is a fine and necessary branch of healing, but it cannot set a man free, just as medical healing cannot set him free. It can set him free—to make his choice, the same choice which doctor and psychiatrist also must make. Who and what can set him free?

IV

In answer, beyond necessity and freedom, history is Dialogue, not between God and the Devil as Toynbee from time to time makes surmise,[27] though there may be conversations in other ranges of being which we cannot overhear, but between God and man. The teaching of history is dull because we have turned history into a monologue: man talking to himself. A monologue is always dull after the first few minutes. Soon it makes no sense. Then history becomes a recitation of successive dynasties, a deadly memorizing of kings and dates and battles. Humanist history has no depth. It is a flatland of man's doings, with no mysterious soundings, no sky, no mountains of mortality to pique our wonder about what lies beyond death. Soon we find patterns in the monologue, for a lonely man repeats himself, and then we think that Arnold Toynbee or (in darker colors) Oswald Spengler has found the answer. Or we comfort ourselves in the monologue—"Now we are getting somewhere"—and then we propose "the inevitable progress of man's mind": the local chamber of commerce sees no reason why every city and every factory cannot get "bigger and better" ad infinitum. The "virtue" of present history is that we can no longer ascribe it to man's monologue. It is apocalyptic: the other Party has broken in upon the monologue, with thunders. He will not let us become blind and deaf in our inordinate self-concern. Oh, for the day when historians will boldly ask, "What does this mean for our history?"!

Can we insist any longer that history is only man's affair? Take the "small" instance. The word "small" is in quotation marks because we do not know what is small or great. Galileo watched the swinging of a lamp in the cathedral of Pisa.[28] This led to the discovery of isochronisms and dynamics. As to the famous telescope, someone noticed that things are seen more clearly through the thickness of glass (in an ancient windowpane?) rather than through the thinness. Did Galileo intend mankind's now wonderful knowledge in astronomy? No, he was half-reconciled to his father's insistence that he become a doctor. A swinging lamp changed both his life and the life of mankind. Then who did intend this portentous change? We cannot ascribe it to happenstance, for the change itself is instinct with purpose. Now take the "large" instance: our present culture which is rapidly becoming one worldwide technological society, in such newness that any doctrine of history as repetition is confounded. Have we intended our nuclear-threatened "civilization"? No, we took our "calculated risks," and made our preparations for defense "in such strength that no one will attack us," blind to the fact that other nations were using the same words, but all the time we intended "freedom and good will." History does not go down our path! Then who did intend our present world? The answer may have been written in one line from a Charles Williams novel.[29] A sentimental lady, who is sure that she is given to piety, says gushingly to the hero of the tale, "Nature is so terribly good"; and he replies, "Yes, terribly . . . a dreadful goodness. . . . Are our tremors to measure the Omnipotence?" Man is not the controlling party in the Dialogue.

God insures necessity, the walls, ceiling, and floors of a room which thus offer us a choice of doors. How does nature remain constant despite mammoth explosions in the "evolution" of vast constellations in a far vaster sky, and despite man's bunglings on the surface of our planet—his cutting down of forests, for instance, to make pulpwood for paper, thus bringing erosion of soil, thus inviting dust storms? How has our planet persisted? Not by our clever hands! How does human life persist, in a society filled with lies—political lies, commercial lies (think of Willie Loman),[30] advertising lies so virulent that we must have defenses such as Consumer Research Reports,[31] ecclesiastical lies (every Sunday morning in suburban churches), lies in the "social set," married lies, academic lies spoken in an impossible "suspended judgment," and the lies we tell ourselves? A sociologist with any depth of vision should know that he is confronting not "laws," but a continuing miracle. That the structure of nature abides, and that the structure of history is held in such firmness that we can study history, is not our doing (how could it be ours?), but sheer grace. The book of Lamentations, of all books, has the truth: "*It is of the Lord's mercies that we are not consumed, because his compassions fail not. They are new every morning: great is thy faithfulness!*" [32]

Meanwhile God insures freedom. Our claim to "scientific discoveries" is deeply stained with pride. The scientist deals with data and that word means "given things." His mind also is given. The structure of nature and of history is also given. Time is given—not in an endless circle which would mock science, but

93

in a straight line of purposeful change, so that hypothesis can lead on to experiment, and experiment to tentative conclusion. How, then, can any "discovery" be mainly man's glory? He could never have discovered it at all unless it were there to be discovered. Wise scientists have again and again cried, not "Eureka!" ("I have found it"), but, "It came to me!", or, "It suddenly came to me." God has instant dealings with us, punctuating His habitual faithfulness. So with the "resolve on freedom": it is not merely our resolve. Take the history of fascist Germany as instance. Who ordained that the Hitler kind of pride becomes blind? Who guarantees that when men become their own law, the gang or tyranny splinters in intermural strife? Who sets a revulsion in the heart of man against such cruelties as were meted out to the Jews in Germany, so that men soon vomit in face of "liquidation"? What is it in us which must oppose such coercion or we inwardly perish? These questions are not about "the laws of human nature." If they were, we might defy the laws. They are questions about the instant and secret word which comes in face of this threat at this juncture. They are questions of Dialogue:

> Go down Moses,
> 'Way down in Egypt land,
> Tell ole Pharaoh,
> To let my people go! [33]

The writing of part four of this chapter began in a quandary: How can I make it clear in a broken and despairing time that history is Dialogue? As I write, as the marks of His overruling and "terrible kindness" multiply and multiply, the question has become: How have we ever become deaf to One who always speaks? Our scientism (not our science) has objectified nature and history and man until the vital subject-term has almost disappeared. But now science itself may be destroyed by its own discoveries as they are perverted by pride, and we must ask, not What is history saying to us?, for "history" soon becomes an

94

abstract term, but, What is God saying to us in the language of event—and of the Event? Above and below the polarities of necessity-freedom there is a Voice and a Hand, not merely through "overruling laws" (that phrase also is abstraction), for history always sets in at single points. What now is the word-event of Him who is over against us, yet within us? Is it not appalling that any co-ed should be taught that history is our domain, soon to be brought under our control by "laws of probability" which our minds can trace? History begins, continues, and ends in Mystery. It is equally appalling that we should think that we can print our patterns on history, our pathetic cycles, and our equally pathetic "progress"—staircases, going where? Our patterns, like ourselves, are contingent and doomed to die.

V

As for Jesus, was he not under necessity? He was bound by our human "constitution" in that he took our human flesh. He was bound by his structure of history—the rule of the Roman Empire in a conquered land, and by all the strange choices thus presented: to join the underground, to become collaborator, to run away from it all to some Qumran community in some near-by desert, to cultivate a pietism, or—to follow the Dialogue. He was bound by the blindness of his society, in such constriction that he said in words that are pathos and love: "I have yet many things to say to you, but you cannot bear them now." [34] He was bound by a family which did not comprehend him, and by a temple which should have welcomed him but actually plotted his death. He was bound at last by the nails and wood of the Cross. Was any other in history so in bondage to necessity? But he spoke no word to endorse our wretched proposal that human life is "determined."

Was he not free? He is history's only free man. George Bernard Shaw, who was sometimes an eagle-spirit, but often only gadfly, said of Christ: "Though we crucified [him] on a stick, he somehow managed to get hold of the right end of it." [35] That is to say, Jesus found doors in what appears to us to have been al-

95

most a prison. The very Cross became the main weapon of his gentle yet tremendous warfare. Why? All human nature is paradox: we view our own life. There is profounder paradox in Christ's nature. From "our side" he was free because always he obeyed the loving commands of the Dialogue. From "God's side" he is "given" to us as the key to God's language and as the incisive disclosure of God's word: "the Word became flesh." [36] Thus we see in him the only freedom, freedom to fulfill our nature. He conquered all outward necessity, even the bonds of death. He overcomes in us the self-forged inner fetter, the worse bondage: "If you continue in my word . . . you will know the truth, and the truth will make you free." [37] The word "truth" there means the unveiling of God's mystery, not a cafeteria of information as a thousand blind baccalaureate sermons would have us believe. Jesus continues: "So if the Son [God's very unveiling and self-disclosure] makes you free, you will be free indeed." [38]

VI

We have pleaded again that history is the Dialogue between God and man in the language of event, and of the Event. If any reader would have "proof," he can consult the mystery of his own history. Can he say, looking back on his life, "It was all my planning and my doing"? No, "there's a divinity which shapes our ends." [39] The reader is in his city because of a conversation with so-and-so on such-and-such a day. Life has turned on a series of apparently fortuitous events. But in retrospect the "chances" are not chances, for they are woven into pilgrimage. Each event now comes clothed in a certain inevitability in time and space and human story: "There's special providence in the fall of a sparrow. If it be now, 'tis not to come! if it be not to come, it will be now; if it be not now, yet it will come: the readiness is all: since no man has aught of what he leaves, what is't to leave betimes?" [40] "Private" history like public history is Dialogue. Each event has prompted us to ask, "What shall I do now?" Nay, the Hidden One, with whom our real conversa-

96

tions are held, has asked us by each event—and by the Event— "What will you do now?" Sometimes we have sought His guidance, for prayer is the true opening into history. Sometimes we have closed our ears. But we never escape the silent Dialogue.

Then what of present history in the light of the Biblical view, namely, that history is Dialogue. H. G. Wells said earlier in our era, before the bomb fell on Hiroshima, "It is the end." [41] If we take the cyclic view, he could be a true prophet, for our civilization may soon become worldwide, so that if this era dies in its cyclic time, no other can take its place. Then no man shall be here to say "The music goes round and round," [42] for the music will have stopped. If we take the "inevitable progress" view of history . . . but how can we? The Rover Boys accompanied by Pollyanna hardly belong in London when bombs fall, still less in Dachau.[43] History viewed as the Dialogue sheds realistic light on present history. In that view we find no cyclic repetition: God's word is not prisoner of any circle. But neither do we find any certain "progress": God's word is not trapped on an escalator. If the Rover Boys reply, "But surely God will not allow man to destroy himself!", we can but answer from history we already know: "God has allowed us to kill off in two world wars upwards of one hundred million people." The sensible answer, the wisdom of the Biblical view, is this: God began the conversation, God continues it, and God alone can determine when the Conversation shall end.

Of course the Conversation, whenever it may end in transient history, is not ended. Or is it? Everybody dies: every "private" history ends on this planet in a grave. "And after death"? An interesting letter has come, proposing that there may be other human societies in other planets, and that therefore God is not defeated because He has not "put all His eggs in one basket." But we do not know that there are "other human societies"; some scientists doubt it, while some have an open mind. If there are others (we still do not know), they also may be caught in what we now call "the human dilemma"; and is not God "defeated" if He loses any eggs in any basket? But "after death"?

97

We do not know in specifics about "after death," but Christ as clue to the language of the Dialogue, Christ as Resurrection, has opened the door into a world beyond.

We are strangely ambivalent about death. Miguel de Unamuno is right: everyone of us thirsts for life: "Eternity, eternity!— that is the supreme desire! . . . . To be, to be for ever, to be without ending! . . . . thirst of being more! hunger of God! thirst of love eternalizing and eternal! to be for ever! to be God!" [44] We understand the words, except for the proposal that man can be God. Miguel de Unamuno quotes Pascal for support, Pascal who said that indifference to death shocked him, and that the man who has that unconcern "is for me a monster." [45] Both men thus take issue with Spinoza who wrote that the free man thinks of nothing less than death.[46] Yet Spinoza also may be right, if such a "free man" is really free. The truth seems to be that you and I hunger for life beyond death, yet avoid thought of death. Why this ambivalence? There may be a thousand reasons in the strange deep called human nature. But one reason may be this: we know that death terminates for us the conversation called history, and that we must then meet Him "with whom we have to do." We may then almost covet oblivion, for He may ask us: "Why for the love of Christ did you keep giving Me that answer?" As to what the Dialogue tells us about "after death," we must inquire.[47] Meanwhile it is worth noting that our ambivalence about death seems to bear witness to history construed as Dialogue. As I write, there are strange events in Oxford, Mississippi; and I have just heard through television the governor of that state say to a football throng: "I lu-u-ve Mississippi!" What else, whom else, does he love? What is God saying just now in Oxford, Mississippi? We know what we are saying, and we know what our laws say. But—what is He saying?

CHAPTER VI

History as Revelation

Is HISTORY REVELATION? CAN IT BE, THIS TINY EPISODE IN TIME?
How can dust and transience be host to the Mystery? We must
be careful how we tread. No man can even see God and live,
much less track Him down our streets which at long last are all
dead-end streets. I read this chapter, in an earlier now-discarded
form, to a group of theologians, whereupon one of them said
in a sad voice, "I wish I could be sure." Then I knew that I
had been too sure despite my remembrance that His ways are
"past finding out." [1]

I

The word "revelation," as we use it of one another, has several
meanings. First, it is an *event* that reveals, as when we find
through the newspaper that an "upright citizen" has been caught
by the police in a gambling den, or learn that some neighbor
whom we had labeled Scrooge [2] is secretly supporting a needy
family. Then the event is *illumination*: the two instances given
above illumine the manner of human life, our ambiguous nature,
the choices which confront us all, and the darkness of our understanding of the man next door. Then and thus revelation is
newness: "Who would have thought that Sammy So-and-so
would frequent a gambling den?" Revelation is thus an invasion
of our ordered world. Often it makes havoc of our earlier trust.
Then and therefore revelation asks *decision*. We must now take
another attitude towards the man whom we have condemned
as Scrooge. Nay, we must act differently towards him. If we
accept the new light we may have a new friendship; if we deny

99

the light because we have enjoyed our condemnation we may fall victim to our own new hate.

Now let us ask what revelation means in regard to God's self-disclosure. The two instances are not *pari passu*, but the human may yet be a distant parable: Jesus offered that plea: "If ye then, being evil, know how to give good gifts . . . how much more shall your Father which is in heaven." [3] In this higher realm we have an act or event, in God's instance an act which cannot be attributed to human power, such as the creation of the world. Here also illumination: "God was in Christ reconciling the world to himself." [4] Here also is newness: for who would have dreamed that God, who makes thunders His chariot and lightnings His sword, would plead at man's door for reconciliation when man is the culprit? Here also revelation is challenge requiring response and decision. Attitude changes: "I never thought that way about God"; and decision follows, which can be either "I don't believe it" or "Now I cast myself by faith on His love."

II

Nowadays revelation, though we constantly meet it in daily life, is a discredited and even contemptible word when used of God, especially in regard to history. The pessimists who favor a cyclic view of history, taking their cue from the repetitions of nature such as the wheeling of the stars, do not like the word revelation, for, of course, it *is* newness: it cuts every circle. The optimists, who read history as progress, like it even less, for they believe man can manage history by what they call "growing intelligence and freedom," or that history itself is an evolutionary escalator as when they drunkenly exclaim "Give the race another million years!" Arnold Toynbee has an ambivalent mind concerning revelation. Now he has no need of it, for he accepts the cyclic view: civilizations rise and fall; again he has no need of it, for he tells us, history is still an open option, and the turning wheels of civilizations may yet be carrying the ark of the new covenant (he forgets that the ark may also be destroyed and can hardly travel in any event on broken wheels); but then

100

he has need of it, for always backstage he sees such a drama as Goethe's *Faust*, a conversation in the sky between God and the Devil which controls historical destiny.[5] He does not make up his mind. By and large the word revelation is a joke in our time: "sheer indoctrination" or a "pious fancy."

But there are signs of a return. Even to the scientist matter is given; he does not make it. Being given, it reveals the Creator; or, if that word also is unacceptable, the Mystery of Origin. Meanwhile the scientist's own life is "given," including both his mind and the framework within which he chooses to work. Wise scientists have again and again spoken of their discoveries as given: "It came to me." Whence? But there are far more startling reasons for our return to "revelation": history now makes chaos of both the cyclic view and the progressive view. The alleged circle is cut by newness such as man could not have dreamed, crucial newness and demonic newness, and the alleged progress has been overwhelmed in blood and hate. It would be prize understatement to say of our time that man's plans have been confounded. There are thunders at the laboratory door, with lightnings that make a Cape Canaveral blast seem like a firecracker. The common man is wiser both than scientism and liberalism, for he says simply, "Man proposes, God disposes." [6] So we ask again about history and revelation. We cannot prove too much. God can and may allow the outright destruction of history. Where, then, the revelation? But if history is His creation, and if He invaded it in Christ as faith believes, perhaps it is a fair assumption that history, though always punctuated by apparent forsakenness, may yet be the place of His self-disclosure.

III

We turn now to the mystery of the event, of any event and of the Event. The event is the hiding place of truth, for the strange wonder of history is in the words, "It came to pass." The word "happen" is rooted apparently in the Old Norse *hap*, meaning luck or chance; and the word "event" springs from the Latin *eventus*, meaning "to come out." Both words acknowledge a

101

mystery: an event is the child of the Totality. Why have we tried to shrink truth to our "telling the truth" ("the truth, the whole truth, and nothing but the truth"!), when we cannot read either our neighbor's life or our own, and when in fact even our eyes and ears may deceive us? We should try to tell the truth, but our telling is still only approximation. Why have we equated truth with scientific truth when science is prisoner of its own framework, the study of a fraction of the world (the natural order) by a fraction of the mind (the rational and analytic mind)? Why have we identified truth with philosophical truth, encouraging students to pursue a mirage called "a true philosophy of life," when philosophy also is limited—to abstractions and the spectator stance? To speak thus is no disparagement of either science or philosophy: it is simply to say that they cannot capture the wholeness and the startling onset of truth. Truth, we have already proposed, is not scientific or philosophical or theological, for it is not in the private custody of man's mind. It is existential through history. Not *in* history, for history is but a tiny and transient episode. God is not domesticated by the historical process, and proud transience can never corral Christ: truth is through history to challenge man in the wholeness, unity and cruciality of his existence; and to require of him a willed venture of response, not merely an aloof stance and a clever mind. If someone says, "This notion would revolutionize the college curriculum," the answer is, "Of course."

So an event is no simple thing. It is revelation. It is therefore, first, event ("It came to pass"), a happening, never mere theory. Then it is illumination: the European common market, a policy in response to events, casts light on man's path, as when we say, "It is clear now, as we should have known, that the economic life of a continent cannot be fettered by national bonds." Then it is newness: it goes beyond man's projects and anticipations, for events cannot in their fullness be causally described. They are flashes of light, not similar links in a chain. Then it is challenge, an appeal to the will, nay, a demand which when rightly met leads to fuller light and act-integration, but which when disobeyed brings desolation. In science we try to subsume the particularity of the event under "laws" which worship sameness; in philosophy we try to hide the unique event under abstractions such as "pluralism" or "empiricism." Both pathways are valid if they help us to return to the actual onset of life with fuller wisdom, but both are under the sovereignty of the event, as when the scientist or the philosopher is born and dies. In religion we do worse: we propose a syncretism which obscures particularity, and thus becomes an outright escape from life: the lowest common denominator! Universals are passive; the event is active. That is why we reckon our mortal days by dates, by events. That is why faith in Christ has its taproot in the Event.

Is not every man's life and the life of society directed by events? We think we think, and then by our thinking shape events, but it is much truer to say that history kicks us in the shins and then we begin to think in order to act: "What now shall I do?" Events sometimes fulfill our human guess, but more often they cut across our plans. This E. G. Collingwood by and large admits, but then he says, "There are no forces other than this activity"—i.e., "the activity by which man builds his own constantly changing historical world"—"which control and modify it." [7] To which the only necessary answer is this: has any man's private history gone down his road, and has present world history honored our "calculated risks"? No, "it came to pass." The U-2 falls, and asks us to grapple more realistically not only with the whole question of espionage, under military order on the eve of a crucial peace conference, but with the whole gamut of world politics. A word is spoken in a casual conversation, and a new job follows which sends a man and his family to the other side of the world. "You may see a stranger across a crowded room," [8] and thus courtship and marriage. Simon of Cyrene, thinking only of the great festival of the Passover, comes into Jerusalem by one gate instead of another, and stumbles on a gallows procession, so that soon he, a stranger in town, finds himself carrying Christ's cross.[9] A fence rail is brought into a political convention, and thereupon Lincoln is elected, and destiny is newly laid on our land. Why do we lavish so much thought on the cyclic world of nature, and so little on history which is always invasive, always paradigmatic, and always unique?

IV

So to our central question: are there certain dominant events in history, and certain reiterations (each with a new thrust) which reveal the ways and intentions of God, and thus disclose our duty and destiny? We tread with care. Events do not necessarily clarify our mind: often they confound our mind. They do not always justify human hopes: often they ruthlessly break human hopes. In toto they tell us that man can never find a home in history. Events do not necessarily reveal God: they may wring from us an agonized cry, "Oh, that I knew where I might find him!" [10] There is a sense in which history always leaves us in dismay, so that a too dependent study of history makes historicism our cruel god. Individual events plunge us into darkness as when a tiny piece of metal is thrown up by a lawn mower which a father is using, and pierces his child's temple. Constellations of events baffle us: the Russian heresy, though it confronts (not evades) the question of property in a technological culture, yet appalls us by its denial of the limits of human power (its flouting of the Sovereignty), and by its attempt to reach an impossible heaven-on-earth through a human slaughterhouse. Yet since God made history and "saw that it was good," [11] it is fair presumption that history has "broken lights" of Him. These we now try to trace, acknowledging in the task that always they involve our act of faith.

There is centrally for Christian faith the total Event of Christ. It is "right" in that Christ is set in the midst of history. He, as climax of covenant history, is by Biblical faith a history within history, a secret history by which general history gathers meaning. He is an Event, not a more discerning Origin of Species,[12] not a new Critique of Pure Reason,[13] not even a sharper Critique of Practical Reason[14] (since Christian faith cannot be reduced

104

to a code of ethic), but a Happening: "Now the birth of Jesus Christ *took place* in this way." [15] The Event is in history. Is He also from beyond history? This question we have not evaded.[16] There is some "evidence," if the works of God can ever yield to that kind of guarantee. The skeptic and the tyrant alike date their letters from his birth, surely not by man's avowed intention, for man's pride has always tried to make its own calendar. His Cross, on which he was helpless (was he?) before the sins of men, now is set against our skyline, though it is a constant rebuke both to our egotisms and our hopes of heaven on earth. But there are no arguments to "justify the ways of God to men":[17] He makes possible and overwhelms all arguments.

The question is not philosophical, but existential. We know that the world was created. How do we know? Not by scientism, but by the painful knife-edge of our own finitude; and that is why, when some scientist speaks to us of some vague "origin of matter" ages ago, we still trust the dismay of the creature. The Biblical avowal of the Creation is not scientific "explanation," but an existential truth. Jesus lived above our constitutional anxiety, though sharing it. He refused every form of our mortal pride. He asked no home or marriage, but had "nowhere to lay his head." [18] He coveted no status or empire: "My kingdom is not of this world." [19] He aspired to no righteousness that could become self-righteousness, but made common cause with sinners, and said meanwhile, "no one is good but God" [20]—which may be why we call Him "good": "Good Master." [21] He yielded even breath at the last: "Father, into thy hands I commit my spirit." [22] He lived in the frustrations of our world, and asked no anodyne. The question, not rationalistic, but existential, not of His nature alone, but of our history, is this: Does He lay on us a claim, in judgment and mercy, which we cannot equate with the claims of men? Does His Deep speak to our deep both in pleading and in power? The "proof" is in that question and in the faith.

The Great Event is "right" both in its brave thrust and its accepted suffering. As to the thrust, Jesus said, "The kingdom of

God is at hand." [23] The Greek phrase could mean also "is within you" or "in your midst." The deciding factor in such alternatives is not etymology, but the whole nature of the challenge of Christ. He is not to be construed by any mystical humanism: he was and is radical confrontation. How have we dared to translate the angels' Christmas song into "peace on earth among men of goodwill"? [24] Do we think we are such, in a generation that made the earth wet with blood and hollow with graves? Men of genuine goodwill would need no Christmas. In this instance the Greek phrase is clear enough, and it does not support our heretical self-assurance: "Glory to God in the highest, [for] there can now be peace on earth, [because] He has shown towards men His [incredible] good will." Bethlehem is the outright thrust; Calvary followed by the Resurrection is accepted suffering and its denouement. Calvary is also "right," for it is that kind of world, and history is itself tragic. All suffering is apocalypse, but often the light is choked: a gangster's death brings no light, especially if we remember our share in his crimes. The death of Saint Joan is of another kind. The light, the cleansing (catharsis was the word applied to Greek tragedy-drama), seems to be in proportion to the obedience of the sufferer. Then what of His death who refused all our idolatries, yet accepted all our pain and shame? Is He history's fount of cleansing? The answer cannot be academic; it is existential.

Thus the "rightness" of the Great Odyssey. History often seems a palimpsest. It is writing on the lines and between the lines and across the lines, with more writing in all directions superimposed on other writing. Often the sentences seem contradiction. Sometimes they shock our hopes, and mock our prayers. But one sentence shines clear. It is stark realism, but men read it with tears and laughter. We push that page aside, for it rebukes our life; but when our life turns sour, we return to that page. The other sentences quiver in light from that sentence, and the whole book begins to gather meaning. So T. S. Eliot tells us perceptively: "A moment in time, but time was made through that moment: for without the meaning there is no time, and that moment of time

106

gave the meaning." [25] Notice the word "meaning." He does not say, "explanation," for an explanation, if ever such a word could be used of history, is always a dead end; but "meaning," though by nature it lives at the heart of Mystery, is "a light to my path." [26] W. H. Auden offers the same insight in other words:

But here and now the Word which is implicit in the Beginning and in the End is become immediately explicit, and that which hitherto we could only passively fear as the incomprehensible I AM, henceforth we may actively love with comprehension that THOU ART. Wherefore, having seen Him, not in some prophetic vision of what might be, but with the eyes of our own weakness as to what actually is, we are bold to say that we have seen our salvation.[27]

The central self-disclosure of God in history and through history (history is not God's prison) is "the Word . . . made flesh." [28]

V

Now we may ask about God's other self-disclosures in our human saga. We must admit that we know them, not as we study history with spectator eyes, for to such eyes they are often hidden, but as we come to history through the Great Event. This admission is not made grudgingly, but joyously and with constant gratitude. Sometimes even the light in Christ seems unable to pierce history's darkness, until we return to the Cross, while at other times the ways of God in history seem clear even to earth-favoring eyes.

History shows the doom of all idolatry. Men cannot absolutize any human artifact or plan without coming on darkness. The word is, "Know that the Lord is God indeed." [29] When we make an idol of color or race, men of other color and race rise in protest, even to the pitch of racial war. Their rebuttal is in mixed motive, for no human motive is pure, but it has worthy instigations, namely, the awareness that a man is a man, with power to view his own life, a center of freedom, a subject who cannot be treated as mere object by some other man's contempt

107

or proud power; for each man's true home is beyond finitude and egotism. Similarly we try in vain to make an idol of cash. Jesus called it mammon.[30] This idolatry in our time has become worse than taxed semi-poverty: it has aroused the envy of the poor, which here and there has become open bloodletting. Marx himself was carried on the tides of hopeless poverty striking back at the rich in bitter retribution. In recent history the victors in war must subsidize the victims or risk worse war; or within the bounds of a nation, when the comfortable have no care for the disinherited, the comfortable must pay for jails, hospitals, police systems, insurance claims, and mental institutions, the same money which might have rebuilt slums and ghettos. Meanwhile our idolatry of gadgets, which lavishes skill on "devising the perfect refrigerator" [31] (which is always out-of-date), leaves us with earthbound minds, as also with less and less time or inclination to fashion a worthier community and a truer church. Gadget-minds cannot understand the profundities of Scripture; gadget-minds can furnish modern houses, but cannot stay the onset of divorce in modern homes. Thus our shrinking world is less and less a neighborhood.

The reader may continue the list of idols if he has the heart. Perhaps learning belongs in the list, for perhaps an academic community may itself become an "acquisitive society," greedy for fact and knowledge instead of for stocks and bonds; nay, no longer a *collegium* (a group of colleagues older and younger under the constraint of truth by faith), but a capitalistic competition in grades and degrees. Then learning is a city in darkness because the lines of communication are cut, the darkness being academic pride with its inevitable jealousies and its contempt for "religious indoctrination": that, and living without any real reason for living. Idolatry is devotion to man's transient rather than for God's Transcendent. As for the modern idolatry of state and empire, our new time has newly marked its new doom:

Imperious Caesar, dead and turn'd to clay,
Might stop a hole to keep the wind away.[32]

If empire does not fall by its own overreaching power, it rots within by self-indulgence, or it rouses rival empires, and with blinded judgment falls with them in destructive strife. History proclaims the doom of idolatry, but only to men with a long look and with eyes cleansed by the central revelation in Christ.

What other light does history give? That God makes known His way and will through prophets who first break with custom and then through martyrdom give their word new power. They first break with custom. Humanistic theories of conscience— that it is an "old wives' tale," or deference to the public mores, or vestige of a child's fear of his parents—all break on the rock of worthy change. The Freudian doctrine of conscience [33] cannot possibly explain Freud's own seeing that the rightful ego should not be slave either of the id or of the super-ego in a coercive and conservative society. Conscience, if that is the right word, is colored by many factors, but ultimately determined by none of them. Conscience means to know with: to know with a world which holds our world in judgment. Abraham leaving Ur of the Chaldees (not as "divine adventurer," but under Covenant command) to seek a city with foundations; Moses leading his people from bondage to a land of promise (not by human wisdom, but because a Voice said, "I have seen the affliction"),[34] Jeremiah under the same Voice seeing in forecast the worth of individual man; and at length all foreseeings coming together in One who said, "The word which you hear is not mine" [35]— such is the blazing of the trail by which man travels, and which he forsakes to become lost in a haunted wood. History moves in response to the prophetic voice or is darkened as men refuse to follow. Thus to speak does not point to nature cyclicism, but to the fatefulness of human freedom.

We must pause here lest we offer too confident a reading of history's pages. Many a prophet dies unknown. He finds acceptance only when the strange tides of history move in his direction. Luther was effective where Hus partly failed. Why? When Hus lived the "time" had not come, whereas Luther's

109

"time" conspired with Luther's word. Thus the enigma of history, which always rebukes our glib reading. Is it not strange that nobleness prevails only when half-noble people, and even unworthy people, unwittingly combine to make currents which carry the prophet on his course? Plekhanov is not totally wrong when he argues that social forces "make" the great man, but he is wrong in his blind denial of the fact that the prophet defies any social force,[36] yes, and any purported dialectic in history: "Here I stand: I cannot do otherwise." [37] A conversation between Kagawa and Gandhi is reported as follows, though I do not know if the report is authentic. When Kagawa asked Gandhi what strategy of peace he should follow in Japan, and Gandhi answered to recommend his policy of nonviolence, Kagawa rejoined that if he tried it he would promptly be dropped from a battleship at night far out at sea.[38] The passivity of Indian thought helped Gandhi, while the militarism of Japan would have thwarted the same policy in Kagawa. All of which is to say that historical decision has always a measure of ambiguity. We glibly propose that what our age needs is "a great leader." But he might not even be recognized, let alone followed; and if he were followed, he would still fail if the crosscurrents of our time did not gather to carry his vessel on his course. The Bible says of Jesus that he came when "the time is fulfilled." [39] He himself said, "My hour has not yet come." [40] Then he said, "The hour has come." [41] God's time does not coincide with either our clocks or our urgent intentions. Again and again history seems to be a Sphinx. Yet it seems true that history is guided by the prophet's thrust.

But the prophet gathers power only from his measure of suffering and martyrdom. The martyrdom [the Greek word, martyr, means witness] may be by sword or gibbet, or it may be by quiet acceptance of failure. Toynbee sees this movement in history, but his thrust of a new civilization and his creative acceptance of a civilization's decline seem often only historicism and sometimes only naturalism—as if changes come only from some historical id; and his whole account gives too little weight

110

to one man and his event. Carlyle was nearer truth when he proposed that history is the lengthened shadow of great men,[42] but he was too little aware of the counterplay of social forces and the ambiguities of historical decision. Do we believe that power comes from brave failure? The New Testament says of us and Christ that we must know "the fellowship of his sufferings."[43] It speaks also of our being "baptized into his death."[44] But we allegorize these sayings, giving them any meaning except the plain meaning which flatly rebukes our cult of prosperity and our pride of "success." Then we justify our condemnation of the prophet, and say with Caiaphas that it "is expedient for you that one man should die,"[45] if need be, than that our "way of life" should be upset. But does not history say repeatedly that light comes through the prophetic man whom we honor only after we have martyred him and garlanded his grave? But maybe we see history thus only because we see it through Christ. If so, we are not confounded.

Again, proceeding warily and confessing that history may now and often mock our surmise, history is the adumbration of a justice below and above our justice and injustice. Our justice is "straight from the shoulder and no nonsense," namely this: the good man should prosper in the earth, with long life and a happy home, while the bad man should be cut off pronto in misfortune. History's bank simply does not honor that check. That is why the Bible, from the insight of Job to the cross of Christ, goes counter to the Deuteronomic doctrine from which our easy notion of justice is descended. Earthly prosperity waits often on the sharpster and the tyrant, and conversely cancer knocks on the door of the godly as well as of the ungodly. The path of suffering sometimes seems wanton and even demonic, as in the instance of the man whose seven children were killed in a railroad crossing accident, and whose wife soon after died in childbirth. Our notion of "equal" retribution or reward is not altogether unworthy, though always somewhat earthy, but it is not fulfilled.

111

We must pause now to remark that our demand that nature and history should be "just" is all too confident, for it forgets our own injustice. How much do we deserve from God? We are self-centered much of the time with scant concern for our neighbors' troubles. Even in conversation we think mostly of ourselves. As for the Mystery in Whom our life is held, we ignore Him: we are earthbound, though always with some vague awareness of "the shadowy third." [46] So we know little about God. Then what "justice" may we rightly ask?

> Though justice be thy plea, consider this—
> That in the course of justice none of us
> Should see salvation.[47]

Yet the fields are fair and fruitful. They demand our labor, for the planet is mountain, desert, and sea rather than field; but the very labor is boon, lest the mind in our precarious life should feed on itself. Rightly we regard the beauty and bounty of the world as "providence"; rightly we regard our homes and the solace of human love as the gift of God. This vast treasure our injustice does not deserve.

But we are here concerned with the adumbration of a deeper justice when our justice seems mocked. For most of us it is little more than adumbration, a darkened token, though for the saints it may be their very life. Here is the hint: is our "good fortune" really good if it makes a man hard and selfish? Does our "misfortune" really miss if beneath it a man becomes sympathetic and learns to trust God? Nature is not always harvest fields, for sometimes it is blight; and even Edna St. Vincent Millay's autumn leaf

> Lord, I do fear
> Thou'st made the world too beautiful this year [48]

was sign of nature's closed circle of life-decay-and-death. History can be more harsh than nature, as witness agelong oppression

112

and war. Yet history shows that when a man bows his head before injustice, when he offers his sorrow as oblation, light breaks in him, yes, and through him for all men's hope. Moreover his foothold is made sure in an unseen world. Negro spirituals are for witness, not least that song which begins in honest confession that history can be harsh, "Nobody knows de trouble I see," and ends with as brave a line as literature could ask: "Glory, Hallelujah!" [49] Below and above man's justice and injustice, beyond and within his always frustrated attempts at "equality," there is the outworking of another Justice. Perhaps that is why we speak of calamity as "an act of God." The mighty are cast down from their thrones, and the meek inherit the earth. But such is the face of history that we can never be sure: we walk by faith. Maybe the avowals of this paragraph are also deductions not from history, but from Christ. But, then, it is our plea that only by His history can we interpret all history, and gladly live within it.

We may instance one other revelation of God in history: the portent of the Church. Here, again, we must write not in brash certainty, but in trembling certitude, for the Church in its present form may be destroyed; and, but for the secret grace of the lowly, may deserve destruction. Yet it is a portent for wonder that there should be in history (as its central and binding thread) a people who are "the new Israel." They began in the old Israel, the covenant folk who dwindled to a "remnant," and then found new focus in Christ. Old Israel was commissioned to make known the name of God, that is, His nature revealed in "His mighty deeds," [50] the deliverance of Israel from wilderness and sea. The new Israel is similarly chosen, the "acts" now being the deliverance of all mankind by means of Bethlehem, Calvary, and a defeated Tomb. All this seems "religious illusion" to modern man with his thin and constricted definitions of "truth."

But the Church persists, in spite of persecutions. Its foes have had the thrones and the powers, the hammers and the anvils,

113

the cash and the swords: in cannibal islands, the Church should have been swallowed, but she persists. She persists, in spite of music which often has been saccharine, hymns which have often been doggerel, and architecture which has often been an affront. She persists in spite of inner, and therefore much worse, deformities—her betrayal of the Lord whom she professes to worship and follow, so that in our time the "Christian nation" anywhere is actually just Christian enough to be troubled by its own paganism, and the Church is just Christian enough to be innoculated against any real commitment. She persists, so that Christopher Dawson can write: "She has been the guest and the exile, the mistress and the martyr, of nations and of civilizations and has survived them all." [51] If he were not Roman Catholic he might more readily add that the Church has persisted in spite of herself. Somewhere there is the story of a man who, acknowledging all the rampant hypocrisy of the Church and all the gibes of his skeptic friends, yet decided to join the Church—because a company so cankered could not have survived unless God in Christ were in her midst!

Should we say with Arnold Toynbee that the Christian faith is carried on the wheels (the cyclic round-and-round) of rising and declining civilizations? This is his escape from Spengler's cyclicism; this is his deference to the Biblical doctrine that man is a pilgrim in and through history. His metaphor of wagon and wheels has some poor light to offer,[52] but it raises questions. Can the precious cargo go forward if all the wheels break and rot? Moreover would any worthy faith, not to speak of faith in Christ, wish so to travel? The wheels are people like ourselves. Would a good God use people as wheels? Would we, who too quickly claim the discipleship of Christ, wish so to be carried, since Christ has told us of the unique preciousness of the person, even of "the least of these," His "brethren"? [53] Moreover, what guarantee is there that any form of the faith known to us shall not perish? The New Testament frankly faces that bleak possibility: "Nevertheless when" he "comes will he find the faith on

114

the earth? [54] The writer feared that all the followers of Christ might be slain!

All we can say with realism is that the Church thus far has persisted, and that the heart of the Church has worshiped God in the midst of history's thousand idolatries, thus saving the world from a complete narcissism; and that the Church within the churches has measurably shown forth the love of Christ amid the world's destructive hates; and that by the attendant grace of God the Church has again and again been renewed in the midst of her own defections; and that the Church, ever confessing and adoring the Mystery of God, has saved human learning from its intellectual pride; and that the Church, aware of its weakness, still cries in the tensions and ambiguities of history, "Even so, come, Lord Jesus!" [55] But to say this is surely to acknowledge the continuing revelation of God in our human story.

VI

This chapter has dealt mainly with the larger and more "public" self-disclosures of the Divine purposes, though in our consideration of a hidden "justice" we have entered the area of more "private" concern. Actually revelation is by nature private. It does not shout to the crowd through a megaphone, though sometimes a crowd is brought under judgment, as when it slinks away after a lynching. No, the individual is self-transcendent in sharper measure than the crowd: the lonely man speaks the prophetic word. That is to say, revelation whispers each man in the ear. The event strikes him, then casts light over the earth, then makes a new world of experience, and then requires of the man his response in obedience or denial.

Thus even "large and public events" have a private reverberation in each man's life. The revolution in Cuba might be the instance. It has individual and unique onsets. This man has business interests there, this man has a daughter teaching in a Cuban missionary school, this man wonders how he can now buy his favorite Cuban cigars, this man fears for the supply

115

of sugar in his coffee; and this man, struck by guilt, remembers how once years ago he took shabby advantage of a Cuban. This last cited man is especially significant, for guilt and penitence are the opening into a deeper understanding of the historical process. The Cuban questions then multiply for each man. These: Why did our State Department support a bloody dictator such as Batista, and what about my vote? What wages were paid by our great commercial firms in Cuba, and what interest did they show in Cuban welfare, and what about my stocks and bonds, and the firm for which I work? How faithful was the Church in Cuba, and what about my church? What groups in the earlier Cuba now comprise the refugees in Florida, and what is my obligation towards them? What depth and hopelessness of poverty drove Cuban peasants to follow a man who cannot say anything effectively unless he rants for hours over the radio: is he better or worse than painted, and what shall my voice say regarding national policy now that Russia is taking Cuba under a Marxist wing? What am I doing about poverty in Cuba or the Orient or in my hometown? Thus public revelation is private, and private revelation is public.

The historian cannot address himself sharply to this individual concern. The "old lady," called history, who "lives in a shoe," called space and time, has "so many children" that the historian doesn't "know what to do." He can only skim the surface of the odyssey of man on this planet. He deals with "issues" and "movements" rather than with John Smith and Joe Brown. But if the truth is existential, not abstract and scientific, John and Joe are host to the truth. Is it not strange that history is both a public concern (the United States now confronts the fact that another economic system can bring both increased "prosperity" and scientific advance) and a private onset? Each man, including the historian, has a unique Morse code by which he construes the apparent generality of the public event. Faith in Christ confesses both the preciousness of each man and "the beloved community" called the Kingdom of God!

VII

Augustine seemed at times to despair of history: "As far as this life of mortals is concerned, which is spent and ended in a few days, what does it matter under whose dominion a dying man lives, if they who govern do not force him to impiety and iniquity?" [56] But, of course, that last phrase is a very large "if," and requires of faith in Christ some brave witness in history. Karl Löwith, as searching a mind in the deeper study of history as our time is likely to find, writes almost in gloom as to our hope and faith: "Perhaps both grow only on the ruins of all-too-human beliefs and expectations, on the fruitful soil of despair of what is subject to illusions and deceptions." [57] But this also does not seem to be the mood of the New Testament. If God in love for men invaded history, and if Christ lived and died in history and then convinced His followers of His presence with them beyond death, what right have we to think of history as hopeless? History is itself contingent, and our minds themselves are both mortal and caught in self-concern; and therefore we cannot print on history any sure pattern, either the pessimism of the cyclic view or the false hope of the progressive view, much less shape history to our plan. Nevertheless "the Word became flesh and dwelt among us." [58] Therefore we may not curse history, but ourselves dwell in it as pilgrims in his light.

Meanwhile we have the clue to history in Christ and his covenant history: clue, not explanation. His spirit abides, and becomes our interpreter. We worship him, thus being "open" to his continuing revealings. Then, since events under His Event are always ecstasy in the fine original sense of the word, namely, that which obliges us to stand outside our life to view it, and to ask "What now am I required to do," we try to do His will in history, not despising either the human pilgrimage or the natural and historical order which is its terrain (for He himself has been pleased to share the strange journey), but walking in His steps who alone could open up "a new and living way." [59] History is revelation even to timebound eyes, and brighter revelation to those who view history from within the faith. Though honesty obliges us to confess that "the whole world lieth in wickedness," [60] not without our share in the guilt, we nevertheless say in New Testament faith:

And we know that the Son of God has come and has given us an understanding, [of history] to know him who is true; and we are in him who is true, in his Son Jesus Christ. This is the true God and eternal life. Little children, keep yourselves from idols. Amen.[61]

Revelation is in and through events and the Event. It is the "sound" of God's voice in the Dialogue between God and pilgrim man; and the Dialogue is called History.

CHAPTER VII

History and Tragedy

THE WORD TRAGEDY COMES FROM THE GREEK *tragos* (GOAT) AND *oide* (song), and points to the practice by which singers in Greek tragedy wore goatskins. These, knowingly or unknowingly, were witness to the cleft which always marks tragedy. Man is in the natural order (as in a goatskin), but not of it. The dictionary gives us some guidance. It tells us that tragedy is a set of events or a literary composition in which the leading figure is "brought to catastrophe" by some "passion or limitation." As for a set of events, recall the history of the Fascist regime in Germany climaxed by Hitler's death in a fiery cellar. As for a literary composition, consider Antigone: [1] the law required that her traitor brother's body be left exposed to carrion birds and man's indignities, but her love required that the corpse be given decent burial. There the cleft was between the "justice" of the state, and the "passion" of filial love. Can there be great tragedy except as history is seen under great dimensions? The "Electra" has nobility because it has noble figures. But what of Mourning Becomes Electra? [2] It has pathos, but, because its people are small and psychotic, it lacks any towering onset.

I

With gratitude to the dictionary we consider "passion." History is swept by passion. The phrase is accurate: passion may be, or may not be by man's engendering, but he cannot domesticate it. Sexual passion carries many a man and woman beyond both wisdom and honor. The passion of political revolution goes beyond itself to kill such a man as Sydney Carton, and to

119

grant room to the bloodlust of the Defarges.[3] The passion for power in church or state disfigures history, even though the Soviet Union in its "scientific" childishness does not reckon with it, even though our American progressivism also is sometimes blind. The suicidal movement of the power impulse is obvious:

> Lo, all our pomp of yesterday
> Is one with Nineveh and Tyre! [4]

but we are victimized in every age. No need to continue the bill of particulars, such as the passion of nationalism which may have carried Judas to his crime. There are passions in a higher register: between man and woman in married troth, between parent and child, between patriot and country, and (strange portent) the passion of the saint for God. But there is need that we mark closely the Biblical view of passion: the admixture of guilt is never forgotten. Man is not the plaything of a pantheon or of fate: he is in the hands of God. Even if he becomes an Oedipus, involuntary slayer of his father, unwitting agent of incest,[5] he knows that he can say either, "Not my will, but thine, be done," [6] or "My will, not Thine, be done." This Job knew, even though we may say that his ills came only from "natural calamity."

As to the other word, "limitation," every passion breaks against the wall. Human freedom is set in the midst of necessity. The passion to know is thwarted by mystery. The yearning of love is mocked by calamity, as in any fatal accident. Think of plague and earthquake as limitation on our builded cities and our still more soaring hopes. The longing for life must meet inexorable death. That was Cleon's tragedy:

> Say rather that my fate is deadlier still,
> In this, that every day my sense of joy
> Grows more acute, . . .
> While every day . . .

My hand shakes, and the heavy years increase . . .
The consummation coming past escape.[7]

Even the passion of the saint for God must walk through "the
dark night of the soul" [8] where God seems a nothing dwelling
in nowhere. Our present history is shadowed by millions of
"displaced persons." But every man is "displaced": his wings
seem caught in nets of steel. Thus writing we must not be blind
to the Bible's characteristic stance: a man's worst limitations are
those built by his own creaturely pride. But for these handicaps,
the other limits might seem like mountains round a fairly
pleasant land, which add mystery and majesty to our mortal life.

"Passion" and "limitation" are scored into history. Johann
Gottfried Herder confronted both. As early as the mid-eighteenth
century he refused the mirage of a neat "science of history."
Honesty saved him from such conceit:

What fate was it, that subjected man to the yoke of his fellows, to
the mad or foolish will of his brother? Let a man sum up the periods
of happiness and unhappiness of nations . . . : how vast will be the
negative number! . . . A Brutus falls, and an Anthony triumphs; a
Germanicus dies, and a Tiberias, a Caligula, a Nero reign.[9]

Herder came to an almost complete pessimism: only "Violence"
and "Cunning" (he writes the words each with a capital letter,
as though they are twin devils) win any victory. Without com-
mitting ourselves to so drear a verdict we should see with Herder
that history, if viewed from the spectator stance, is tragic; and
we should mark his awareness of the clash between good and
evil. Tragedy lives always in clash: flesh against spirit, freedom
against law, desire against a contradictory world, mind against
enigma, life against death. Even so we should reserve judgment
on tragedy regarded as an ultimate word.

II

The dictionary also summarizes the effect of tragedy on the
man who views it: it "excites pity and terror." To these words

121

we should add a third: catharsis. Consider the fascinating word "pity." It implies that tragedy is out of place in history. Its instant expression is, "What a shame!" The scheme of things should be ashamed! Or it says, "That's too bad!", which could mean, "History ought not to be so corrupted!" Pity, that is to say, has glimpsed another dimension of life. But—to remind ourselves again of the Biblical mind—pity is not always aware of pity's own shame and badness. It pities the victim of tragedy. If it went to help him, pity might be lost in love. So pity, when it is content only to pity, identifies itself with the tragic victim to become self-pity, and self-pity may be the final pride. Or pity becomes a private indulgence of emotion. Is there not somewhere in the Russian novelists the story of a woman weeping copiously over the tragedy on the theater stage while her coachman, waiting for her in the Russian winter, was suffering real pain? [10] So pity easily misses culpability both in the tragic figure and in itself; and, missing that mark, it may close the door against both judgment and mercy. Momentously Jesus on his way to Golgotha refused pity: "Daughters of Jerusalem, do not weep for me, but weep for yourselves and for your children." [11] He would not let them shut their eyes to responsibility.

"Terror," the second word in the dictionary count, may be a nobler word than pity. Its merit is awareness of the Abyss, a recognition of man's constitutional helplessness. Terror has ridden with many a man in a small plane as it has plunged through a piled-up "cold front." Then what of the more unaccountable storms that erupt from below the ground of what we call "normal conduct"? Dachau and Buchenwald [12] are a terrifying portent, though (once again) not without a more terrifying guilt. What of the stark contrariness of history, as seen in the blindness of Victorian optimism to the cleavage that would come with industrialism, to say nothing of the fury of the Russian revolution? What of the central Biblical concern—the rampancy of evil in our world? Evil is not atomized in this man here and that man there: it is organized, and sometimes moves like a violent army. And what about the terror of death? We pretend that death is mere cessation, but its effect is not that of quiet ending, but of shock, of questioning and of judgment. Sigmund Freud assumed that his "science" would one day explain the hidden depths of the psyche, but was himself troubled again and again by thoughts of death.[13] There is honesty in the terror evoked by tragedy: our scientific optimisms are a poor refuge. But can terror be a final word? If so, history is paralyzed, like a bird under the poised fang of a serpent. Pascal declared that he was greater far than any world that might crush him, for he would know he was being crushed.[14] Perhaps terror easily becomes cowardice. Perhaps both pity and terror are cankered by self-interest.

We must add the word "catharsis." The dictionary does not cite it, but Aristotle did: he said that tragedy purges away the pity and the terror.[15] Strange claim! Are pity and terror, then, an inner sickness? Just as psychiatry brings to the surface some suppressed desire, a murderous intent or an incestuous longing, so that it can be skimmed away instead of lurking unknown in the depths, so tragedy finds and washes away the pity and the terror. Thus we sometimes admit to going to the movies to "have a good cry." But again the questions multiply. Catharsis may come to the spectator of tragedy, but what about the tragic victim? There is no guarantee of his cleansing. He may decide that Camus is right in his surmise that all history is "absurd," [16] though Camus was too fine to follow through on his own proposal. He may be utterly crushed, or he may settle on the lees of a dull stoicism:

> For men must work, and women must weep,
> And the sooner it's over, the sooner to sleep;
> And good-by to the bar and its moaning.[17]

There are further questions. Is the catharsis permanent, or must it be repeated? If repeated, how often? Is the repetition healthy, or dangerous as in oft-repeated physical catharsis? Moreover, have we the right to use another man's tragedy for our cleansing?

The word catharsis also may be suspect. Perhaps it should be arrested on charge of false pretenses.

As to these three words—pity, terror, catharsis, the evocations of tragedy, is there not danger that our discussions of tragedy may end as—discussions? Are they not vitiated by a spectator stance which is not given to men? Do they not treat life as if it were stage drama? Do they not evade responsibility, the ability to respond, to an order of life above history? Do they not treat the past as if it were dead, and tragic figures as if they were objects? If so, have we any right thus to regard the sorrows of Lincoln or even the unknown agony of the victims of Attila? Is life fulfilled if we merely look at the Cross, as if it were a spectacle, as if we were not involved, or as if (Nietzsche's appalling proposal) it were occasion for a deeper aestheticism,[18] a picture with more than Rembrandt vividness of light and dark? Perhaps our age in its new awareness of tragedy may fall into that pit. In any event, pity, terror, and catharsis are evanescent. They speak no solving word in tragedy. They may belong to inordinate self-interest and to unfaith.

III

Thus we confront again questions of stance, attitude, and redemption.[19] How shall we regard tragedy? If it is "too bad," if it does not belong, how is the clash of tragedy resolved? Auguste Comte's optimism, that man is on a scientific highroad to perfection,[20] is now exploded, though there are still some people who think Emerson and Whitman are prophets, and try to relegate Hawthorne and Melville to an alleged morbidity. Most people, including the common man, who usually has a more uncommon sense than the philosopher, knows that our world has fallen about our ears. Civilization is a screen to hide a Mystery. We go to business, play golf, watch the stock-market ticker, build a suburban home complete with patio and swimming pool, and so distract ourselves from the ache of asking whence we come and whither we go. This fiction of our daily life is so seeming-solid, so reiterated and encompassing, that we have lost the sense of the Presence. God may once have been with men, and in a happier time men may again be known by Him, but we live in a meaningless interim. We blame Him or deny Him, rather than blame our culture and our own pathetic self-concern. Is not our alienation the evidence of Him, if only by reversion? But the refuge is now broken, and—what to do?

Tragedy breaks all our neat "theories of history." The art and craft of the historian abide. We need him. Nothing in these chapters derogates his gift. We should not require him to be either philosopher or theologian. His task is to tell a story well and bring it to life.[21] But it is still not enough to describe tragedy, if tragedy is the word, for the spectator stance is finally the denial of life. The historian, along with every other man in history, is caught in the clash of freedom and necessity. The past is not past: it lives in the present not only as delineation of the historical necessity in which we live, but as summons to our gift of freedom, and as belonging to that world of vital memory by which we transcend the hurrying years. The historian is himself a man confronting tragedy, especially in its clash of good and evil; and his concern with history is consciously or unconsciously a quest for answer to his own dilemma. So, with gratitude for his gift, he and we must alike say that it falls short. We should not ask him to forsake his historical studies, his work being a form of dramatic literature harbored in what happened, but we must go beyond him for the solving word.

A "science of history" even if it were possible would not be an answer. For science sees only part of a man, his life in a determinate order of nature or of historical necessity; and in the seeing employs only part of a mind, namely, rational analysis. So it is not surprising that positivistic history runs out, like a stream swallowed by a desert, into endless discussions of what is meant in historical study by such words as "cause" and "explanation." Some of us have only proximate interest in these words, for they do not touch the nerve of tragic life. A "science of history" must finally view man as determined; it must deny his freedom. Then there can be no tragedy, for then there is no

125

clash between liberty and law: Antigone is merely going through the motions. It is always possible, and perhaps to some small purpose, to trace patterns in the past—if the past is past, and if men are now objects. But these patterns, even in Arnold Toynbee, are always partial fictions, because tragedy breaks all patterns, and because the historian still lives in the tragic world, as when his parents in Europe become "displaced persons." A science of history becomes cyclic when it takes the order of nature for its cue (as if man were only in nature), and progressivistic when its eyes are on "scientific advance." As to the latter, it is worth noting that the jailors at Buchenwald [22] used "advanced science" to turn their victims into soap.

A "philosophy of history" is no great gain. Dealing in essences and universals, it overlooks the individual man, in whom tragedy strikes, just as the "laws" of science overlook the thrust of the particular event. Philosophy discusses battles and issues (rightly, for there is a socio-economic "structure" in history), but forgets the man killed and the home darkened by grief. It considers dynasties, but not this father now torn from his children. It tells of volcanoes, but ignores the sudden terror of people living in that house on that street in Pompeii. It enlarges on "the refugee problem," but, if it does no more, it has "passed by on the other side" [23] of people sleeping homeless on the hillside above Kowloon. Demands of mind may always require us to seek a "philosophy of history": I do not know. Or should we say, rather, that any true philosophy must have an existential cast? In any event, a philosophy can hardly provide a solving word in man's tragic dilemma. The Bible never turns its eyes from the man. It has no truck with cold neutrality. It does not deny the uses of the wide lens of philosophy, but insists on a close-up also, taken not with a camera, but with a human eye. The close-up shows every man caught in tragedy.

IV

Then what has the Bible to say about the clash of freedom and law, spirit and form, life and death? What is its solving

126

word? It confronts "the tragic sense of life," [24] not to examine
or pity, but in the sharp awareness that if the clash is not resolved
history is slain. Tragedy is lesion: if the lession is not healed,
the victim bleeds to death. The deeper lesion, says the Bible,
is between the pride of the creature and the will of the Creator.
So this Book dares mysteries while other books discuss movements. It looks beyond history to Him who alone can overarch
our agonized polarities. Then what is the word? It is not a word,
but THE WORD. How to tell THE WORD? Tintoretto flung
down his brush before splendor, exclaiming, "I cannot paint
it!" [25] This book is not Tintoretto (would it were!), and the
splendor is now none other than the Shekinah [26] in our mortal
flesh. All our words are now moths consumed in the flame. But
they may thus be a better testimony. In devotion they may find
their true life.

The Bible says that history is a tremendous Dialogue—not
the thin dialectic which Hegel proposed in philosophy, much
less the false dialectic which Marxism has tried to print (with a
rubber stamp of death) on our human story, but a Dialogue
between the Creator and the human creature. This, says the
Bible, is the responsible interchange, and goes far deeper than
any other polarity. There are other dialogues: that in multiple
form within each man; that between man and nature, which
science explores; and that between man and man, which our
various sociologies interpret; but these fainter conversations are
held within the crucial Conversation between man and God,
without which the other dialogues reach no end and find no
meaning.

How do we know? We know. God is not "proved," but takes
us unawares. We can marshal the evidences, but only after
the event. This: we live under obligation. Even in a primitive
tribe the needs-must is not merely on a horizontal line between
man and man, but on a vertical line to some Unknown who is
above both cult and tribe. And this: each event speaks, or would
if we were ready to listen, for each event has an obtrusiveness,

127

a singularity, a from-beyondness which says, "Thou are the man!", thus evoking our praise or shame. The event of the discovery of nuclear fission is saying to our whole generation, "Use this well under the Creator, or perish." Or this: each neighbor, because he also has his secret awestruck Dialogue, may not be used, but must be honored. And this: each man has power to view his own life, so that the great Conversation has its inward home as well as its cosmic summons. And this: beauty is not utilitarian, but its own form of truth. Every man can supply his own "and this." A friend has given me two lines from John Masefield written in ink by the poet's own hand:

> O wet red swathe of earth laid bare,
> O truth, O strength, O gleaming share.[27]

These are the following lines:

> O Jesus, drive the coulter deep
> To plough my living man from sleep.

God's plow does not leave our field long unturned.

As for tragedy, who ordains the necessity and the freedom, and their polarity? They are both within the created order. This we know, for we know beginning and ending, life and death. History, by our very use of the word, by our power to comprehend man's total pilgrimage, is a path of finitude. Then what lies beyond the path? The Dialogue proceeds across

> the gates
> Of saving flesh and bone,[28]

since no world can bar His coming. Every man believes in God, for every man knows responsibility. Every man has his own name for God: Truth, Reality, Ground of Being, The Unknown. When Kierkegaard was asked if he believed in God, he replied: "Why, of course, what else?" [29] There is nothing else. The question is not if God exists, for that question degrades God

128

to the level of an existent, but rather, "What is God like?" The answer must come from God, for no man can climb the sky. It must come in events, for we live in a nexus of meaningful occurrence. Should we not say, then, that man's tragic dilemma finds resolvement, if at all, in a saving series of events and in the Event?

If the first word in the Biblical approach to tragic history is Dialogue, the next is the Piercing Event. The Dialogue is in the language of event. The Biblical claim is that history finds meaning in Christ, and in him is carried beyond tragedy. Every event and every series of events is unique. That is why patterns drawn in history are never better than typologies, reflections of the immemorial human choice, the broken rhythm of man's self-concern and self-surrender. One Event cuts through all patterns: such is the Biblical claim. Christ is clue. Clue is the word, not explanation, for clue calls for courageous faith, while explanation either brings life to a halt or endlessly asks further explanation. "What is God like?" He is not like a scheme of "justice" with an invincible police force; not like the space-time continuum or any other abstraction; not like the vast cosmic holocausts of fire from which new constellations emerge; not like mere pity or mere terror or any temporary catharsis. These are adumbrations of the Abyss. But God is really like a Man dying on a Cross. He is as helpless and as mighty, as vigilant in truth and as utterly self-giving in love. The Church has not always kept faith with this faith: it is too staggering. There is no argument to "prove" the faith: love is not verified by logic, still less God's love by man's logic. There are better questions: Does the Cross find us? Does it silence proud logic? Does it convict us of sin and bring us to penitence? Does it cast light on tragic history?

The history of Israel, Christ's own people, was tension and tragedy. Has Christ resolved that clash? Has he brought that history to fulfillment? The smoke of theological battle gathers round the word "fulfillment," but the cloud begins to clear. We now see that some Old Testament texts quoted of Christ as ful-

129

fillment have been "used" rather than fulfilled: literal minded scholarship has overreached itself. But would literal fulfillment be fulfillment? Would it not rather be echo and repetition? But Bultmann's proposal that Matthew's oft-repeated "that it might be fulfilled" is mainly polemic and "proof-text" brings even less conviction.[30] The mind of Israel, unlike the Greek mind, was not given to polemic. When do the Scriptures argue the existence of God? An "Israelite indeed" [31] was God intoxicated on a far deeper level than Spinoza ("The God-intoxicated man"),[32] for Spinoza philosophised about God, while Israel was beset by God. Matthew's "that it might be fulfilled" is confession, not polemic; surprise and adoration, not argument. It says, "See how the promised joy has come to pass!"

Nor is Bultmann persuasive when he says that Christ fulfilled the Old Testament by "not fulfilling it." [33] What can such a phrase mean except that Christ transformed and redeemed the hopes of his people? Indeed what else could ever be fulfillment? He said, "The time is fulfilled." [34] He said that his death would be "exodus"; "She hath done it for my exodus," [35] for that is the meaning of the word which the King James Version translates "burial." He made new the ancient covenant: "This cup is the new covenant in my blood." [36] The kingship to which Israel looked in hope came to pass in his kingship, which "is not of this world." [37] The promise of a "shepherd" for Israel found actuality in him who laid "down his life for the sheep." [38] The "Suffering Servant" passages ("He was despised and rejected by men; a man of sorrows, and acquainted with grief") [39] leap into piercing light at the Cross. Yes, Bultmann is right in claiming that complete fulfillment is "eschatological," [40] for so is any historical destiny: a finite world cannot find its *telos* in mortality. But the word "eschatological" cuts both ways: if it has no meaning now, what meaning can it have hereafter? Christ gathered the tensions and tragedy of Israel into his own heart. There they found meaning and healing. Hereafter they shall be stamped with heaven's seal.

But what of our tragedy? We are not Bible folk: our time in history is almost ignorant on that score. We are not "God-intoxicated": we confess Him (it *is* confession) only in denial. Only now are we ready to quit our shallow optimisms and admit that history has a tragic cast; only now in strange reluctance, strange because every man's private history leads to griefs and graves. To be specific, what of the central issue (always central in Scripture): the obdurate pride by which men and nations come on desolation? In blunt answer, we cannot heal our self-hurt, or even cleanse our memory. A man speaks sober truth when he cries in contrition: "I can never forgive myself." Much less can we mend the hurt in history, or send the Hiroshima bomb back into the sky, in a world in which even "our echoes roll from soul to soul." [41] There can be a measure of healing and forgiveness from man to man, but only a measure, for we ourselves are creatures: our guilty spear is lifted against creation and the Creator. Only He can heal and forgive and re-create. Only He, *within* history, for only so can men see pardon and accept it; only He, from *beyond* the gate, inasmuch as all history is tragic, and healing must come from beyond history. John Whale tells how his school referred to a nearby ridge of hill with a lone tree against the sky as "the end of the world." [42] Yes, "who his own self bare our sins in his own body on the tree"! [43] The Cross is the end of our world, and the beginning of God's world. Always it stands on the border, where man's proud hopes are broken, and God's new grace is given.

As to our other tragedies, nearer to the surface of life than our tragic disobedience, yet deep enough, they all tell of a cleft in history: spirit held in a prison of form, freedom beating its wings against necessity, the longing for life confronted by the limits of death. Has Christ bridged that cleft? Bible writers, though their central concern was with Bible history, yet had all history in view, as witness such phrases as "all nations" and "the kingdoms of this world." A strange word from Nietzsche provides an opening in this tremendous issue. In his absorbed concern with Greek mythology (what would have happened if he and Freud had begun with Biblical symbols instead of Greek mythology?) he wrote: "Thus do gods justify the life of man, in

131

that they themselves live it—the only satisfactory Theodicy ever invented." [44] It was not "invented"; it was given, mixed in with our human clay. But perhaps, on a deeper level, we do have here "the only satisfactory Theodicy." Ivan Karamazov's bitter protest against tragedy, his declaration that God has no right to plow under even one praying, tortured child for "the future of the race," [45] cannot find answer in any philosophy. Indeed Ivan's sin was precisely his demand for a philosophy, his requirement in rebellion that God play lackey to Ivan's lordly mind. Man is man: he cannot with impunity eat the fruit of the tree of the knowledge of good and evil. Man's life is hedged about by mystery, and his mind also is mortal. Ivan's protest was not wrong: the wrong was in his pride of mind which, incidentally, prevented him from bearing the burden of the tragedy of his neighbors. The protest was proper answer to our windy speeches about "the future of the race," for what do they mean if for every man history is tragic? But if God has justified our life by living it Himself, then indeed we have a theodicy. The Bible points to that piercing event: "The Word became flesh." [46] Surely he, Word of God, "has borne our griefs and carried our sorrows." [47] Thus the deep cleft is bridged. Mystery is still mystery, but now mystery glows with meaning.

Beyond Dialogue (which is the Biblical interpretation of history), and beyond the Piercing Event (which is clue to the Dialogue) stands Resurrection. The Bible view does not offer Calvary as the final word in the Dialogue. Had it been so, history is nothing but tragedy, for the best is at the mercy of the worst, and that is the end of the whole story. We must go further and say that the New Testament points to the Cross only in the light of Easter Day, for only that light enabled Christ's first followers to see God's hand and heart in Calvary. Without Resurrection the Cross is Devil's work, and Christ a tragic victim. What else but Resurrection could have written the New Testament? That Book, which even our largely pagan culture cannot escape, is not a dirge sung round a grave, but a shout of joy around a conquered grave. Our newspapers quote the Book in "A Text for the Day," as if it were a collection of "guidances" or, worse, prudential maxims, but shy away from the tremendous implications of the Cross and the Resurrection which bring all newspapers and all man's doings to judgment and mercy. What else but Resurrection can account for the origin and continuance of the Church? The Pentecost folk fairly sprang on the world, not in the despair of a gallows, as if the whole music had ended in a horrible discord, but in the joy of a victory, because God had brought the music to rest in one great triumphant chord of light. Nor could the Church have survived centuries of persecution and its own acknowledged shabbiness and perfidy in any other power.

The Resurrection also is Event. The form of the Event we may not dogmatically trace. The New Testament itself, which never plays errand boy to our neat logic, which breaks rather into drama and great music, says that Christ came in the very body which had been his on the way to the Cross [48] (thus insisting that they knew his identity), and yet says that "he entered, the doors being shut" [49] (thus declaring that no barrier can now bar his coming). We were not there on Easter Day. The pain of our not being there is reflected in the story of Thomas refusing to believe in the Resurrection unless he (blinded by his eyes) could put his finger in the very wounds of the Risen Christ.[50] The joy of the present Spirit of Christ, and the valor kindled by him, is in the word of his presence: "Blessed are those who have not seen, and yet believe." [51] By whatever form, the Resurrection is Event, not, as Bultmann would have us say, a conjuring-up of the sorrow of those who had witnessed his death on the Cross.[52] Sorrow of itself does not grant such rapture. No, the word is Event. The joy is too sudden in its surprise, the change in the disciples too startling, for any other word. To say of men who on Friday were in despair and on Sunday overwhelmed in light, on Friday dull pupils and on Sunday men who knew now the whole meaning of life, and (the most marvelous change) on Friday men of timid self-concern and on Sunday fearless of death

133

in a new gift of love—to say of such men that they were victims of "illusion" or "projection" does not impugn the New Testament: it proves only that our rational mind can be locked in its own rationality, a tiny dungeon in a cosmic midnight. The only plausible prelude to the Easter joy is Event, namely the quiet avowal of his first followers: "Jesus himself drew near." [53]

The Cross itself is for witness. For what is Calvary now, despite our skepticisms? A gallows, yes, but no longer a gallows. The building astride the south end of Park Avenue in New York City on Christmas Eve has windows left alight to make the sign of the Cross. A gallows, a gas chamber if you will, a lynching, on the eve of Christmas joy! In a building given to trade and the professions! Is that witness, which goes counter to our bourgeois culture, mere sentimentalism? Is the poignant music of the Bach "B-Minor Mass" only "escape"? If not, have we any right to take the music as part of our "culture," and throw into discard the faith that wrote it? Is "The Hallelujah Chorus" a cowardly "projection"? Or are our poor little clichés the prattle of children running for shelter rather than confront the great Dialogue? This transformation of a Gallows is not our doing, for we lead Christ to some new Calvary in every generation. No, the Event is alive, through the power of an abiding Spirit, to "convince the world of sin and of righteousness and of judgment" [54]—in Love slain on a Cross to be raised in victory.

Thus the Cross carries us beyond "pity," "terror," and "catharsis," in short beyond tragedy. Do we pity Christ? Are we terrorized by Calvary? We know now the enormity of sinful pride, but that conviction issues in penitence, not in terror. Do we come to Golgotha to "use" it for some temporary catharsis? No, rather we nod assent when Roland Hayes asks in his plaintive tenor, "Were you there, when they crucified my Lord?" [55] Do we now speak of "passion" and "limitation"? No, for at Calvary we see another kind of passion, the disclosure of God's love for men, which breaks through every limitation, even through the final black limitation called death. We now know "what God is like." God has made clear the sometimes cryptic

134

Dialogue. He spoke the first sentence when we were born and when history began. He will speak the last sentence, for He is God, in history's hidden fulfillment. We now have answer—not in some poor "analysis," but in summons to a living faith—to the questions which always haunt us: "Who am I?" (the question of parentage) and "Why am I?" (the question of purpose and destiny), for God has spoken a middle sentence: "This is my beloved Son: hear him" [56]—the word "hear" in Scripture always carrying deep undertones, not of mere listening, but of glad and obedient response.

V

The convictions of this little book now can be clearly traced. Tragic history when brought to the Event has an answer to "the problem of history." History is not cyclic. If it were, men would not be men: they would be only more complex squirrels in a squirrel-cage. Is it not astounding that we have not challenged Oswald Spengler (yes, and Arnold Toynbee too after his measure), but rather have been ready to surrender all that makes us men? History is not necessary progress. If it were, once again men would not be men, for by that doctrine we would be only dummies riding an escalator. Is it not doubly astounding that we should sell out to that nihilistic optimism? The trouble with both views, with nothing to choose between them, is that they deny the plain fact of our creation and of the creation of the world. They mock our very concern with history, for they flout our strange power to view our world and our life in history. Creation itself, whatever the mystery of God, requires another view of our human story. History is Dialogue: the Conversation proceeds for every man and for all history in the strange language of unique yet related events, with one Event as key to the translation.

As this chapter was being written, a friend, Philip S. Watson,[57] asked, "What is your view of history?" I answered: "It is not mine: I received it through Grace." He persisted: "But what is it?" Then I said: "Cyclicism which is now fashionable and pro-

135

gressivism which was recently fashionable are both the death of freedom, and therefore of any meaning in history. History is Dialogue, a conversation by means of events, between God and men, which honors the strange freedom which God has given." Then his answer, like a quiet thunderbolt, "You mean that the door of hell is always open?" To which I said: "Yes, and the door of heaven." To which he, in persistent insight, said, "Men are willing to believe the door of heaven is open; that may be why they are progressivists. But they blink the door of hell." Another colleague, Samuel Laeuchli,[58] promptly added: "And the Church has sometimes forgotten which door is which." But fatefulness in man's freedom cannot be blinked: events, as in our fateful time, become our theologians.

History as Dialogue, a conversation between God and man, carries us beyond tragedy, but it does not cancel suffering or enigma. It does not provide "explanations." Consider the disaster which our coveted "explanation" would bring on us. It would become "a dead certainty," than which nothing is more dead. It would be a "cut-and-dried" answer, than which nothing is more cut and dried. It would lead the mind into a blind alley, than which nothing is more blind. History is too kind to give us explanations. In the great Dialogue of History, which appears in microcosm in every man's life, suffering is not explained. If it were, it would still have to be met, and would thus reawaken the ancient questionings. What this view of history gives us is a faith by which to meet suffering; and not only a faith, but the power of a living Event, by which suffering itself is transmuted; not explanation, but power and victory, beyond which the questions are answered—or would be, except that then we care nothing about explanation because our little rationalisms are now overwhelmed in light. For instance, we fear no Freudian deeps, for we are engaged in the Great Dialogue. We know that man's nature and history are held in Power which guards all the gates. The hidden dynamisms of our life and history are encompassed by Grace.

136

VI

There is a further word: history regarded as Dialogue rules out the spectator stance. We may not (it is against our constitution) be content merely to pity, or to surrender to terror, or to ask some temporary catharsis. The only vital way in which history can be known as Dialogue, with Christ as the revelatory Word, is that we try to re-enact in our own finite and individual history the clue and thrust of his life. So the New Testament, with insight and courage not given to another Book, speaks of being "baptized into his death" and of rising with Him into "newness of life." [59] We are in history, as he was in history. We cannot be academic spectators, or we ourselves, to quote a phrase which is its own terrible indictment, will become "a merely academic question"! We are involved and cannot flee involvement; and the meaning of history becomes clear by involvement, not by philosophizing; on the field, not in the grandstand. Paul, prodigious mind, whose pastoral letters, tossed off to a scribe for the sake of tiny churches which seemed less than candles in a gusty pagan world, now confound our optimisms and our pessimisms, probing depths which we pretend are not beneath our feet—a pretense which no longer grants us any refuge:— Paul was writing not about some pious little choice, but about all history, yes, and about the way in which private history becomes the clue to all history, when he said as one who had emerged from bafflement into light: "that I may know him and the power of his resurrection, and may share his sufferings, becoming like him in his death, that if possible I may attain the resurrection from the dead." [60]

CHAPTER VIII

The Fulfillment of History

HISTORY CANNOT FIND FULFILLMENT IN ITSELF, EITHER IN "THE American Dream" or in the Soviet Paradise or in some purported evolution. This is a hard saying. It shocks the pride of our generation and deepens our anxiety, anxiety-pride being two sides of one shield. The men of Babel were sure they could build a tower as high as heaven. Pride moved them: "Let us make us a name"; and anxiety prompted them: "lest we be scattered abroad upon the face of the whole earth." [1] But their tower was destroyed long before it reached the sky. The Bible says that God destroyed it. If you prefer another phrase (it is the bane of our age to interpret personal experience by impersonal phrases), it was not according to the *telos*, the ultimate and hidden purpose of the cosmos. We human beings, who believe anything about ourselves except that we are human, always try to "draw a circle premature": [2] to catch history in the net of our own finalities, instead of acknowledging God's *telos*, which, of course, must go beyond history since God is not prisoner of our planet. History cannot find fulfillment in itself.

Need we rehearse the reasons? Here they are, for we should confront the hard saying. History is *in time*, and time carries a scythe. When a new pope is crowned, the priests rightly intone, "*Sic transit gloria mundi.*" History is *paradox*, and the nature of paradox is such that its terms cannot be resolved except in a higher term: the paradox of south and north (it is paradox in a tiny planet spinning like a child's top in the void) requires reference to a point beyond the planet. History is *human*, for it is centrally the story of man's life on earth, and every man dies:

138

that is, all history shares the contingency of our mortal life. History is a little paragraph which gathers meaning only in the light of its whole hidden book of which the Bible says with realism: "no man in heaven, nor in earth, neither under the earth, was able to open the book, neither to look thereon." [3] History is *created*, as man's life is created, and all things or men created are away, yet never away, from the Creator's hand: the beginning and end of creation, which we know existentially from our own finitude, are hidden in the Creative Mystery. Finally history is disfigured. It is both irony and tragedy, and thus can never be its own cure. History cannot find fulfillment in itself. Therefore our theme: The fulfillment of history.

I

We must admit at once that such a theme seems to mock us. It saddles us with the immemorial questions which our humanisms try to evade: "Who am I?" and "Why am I?" Secularism is a conspiracy to sidestep the primal questions. The "who?" asks about the mystery of origin, the "why?" about the mystery of destiny. The one is concerned about the void whence all history comes, the other about the *telos* towards which all history tends. How then shall we, who are in history, hope to pry into the secrets of prehistory and post-history? We are involved in the historical order, caught in the time-space continuum; what can we know of the time beyond time, when the little loop of history shall be gathered back into its proper fabric,

> When that which drew from out the boundless deep
> Turns again home? [4]

There is some answer, though no full answer. For one thing, history bears within itself hints and gleams of its origin and destiny. Its very brokenness points beyond to that which is not broken. Perhaps all relativities imply an absolute. It can be said of history as of our personal life,

139

> our life's Star,
> Hath had elsewhere its setting,
> And cometh from afar:
> Not in entire forgetfulness,
> And not in utter nakedness,
> But trailing clouds of glory do we come
> From God, who is our home.[5]

For another thing, each man's secret life gives him a glimmer of ultimate purpose, for he views himself in time, and therefore has some freehold and foothold beyond time. Furthermore, if our plea has carried persuasion, every event is *aletheia*: it brings tidings of a hidden world. This is true at least in Christian faith, which holds that Christ is the focal and revelatory event by which all events can be construed—not for the mind's curiosity, but for the whole man's venture. The event may fall on blind eyes, but ever and again it pierces our blindness, as when someone said: "War is the truth about our civilization." So there is some answer, though it is always partial and open to worthy doubt, about the fulfillment of history.

But the answer cannot come in the language or thought forms which apply only to our timebound life. We cannot use logic, for logic is in the time sequence and, in any event, rests back on accepted axioms. Logic says: "There were footprints in the mud outside the door, and there was trampled mud inside the door, and the steps led directly to the bed where the sleeping man was murdered." This at least is detective fiction logic. It is in both the natural and the historical order, and we are now concerned with another dimension. By the same token we cannot use science, for science is concerned centrally with the natural order and/or with man's life in that order. Science makes man and his world an object. But man is not merely an object: he does the viewing. God cannot be an object, for, if He were, He would be but another object (however huge) in a roster of objects (however small); and thus could not be God. The Russian astronaut [6] who informed us that he had not seen God anywhere during the

140

sputnik flight may be well-versed in science, but he is a kindergarten child in any wisdom. Logic may adumbrate a higher order, for it must accept axioms; and science may hint the Uncreated as often as it speaks of the created, for to draw any circle is to confess a mystery beyond the circle; but neither logic nor science is now our proper medium. Do we not speak of "cold logic" and "dispassionate science"? Our life is neither cold nor dispassionate; we long for some answer. Mark therefore that we are moved by picture, such as the Raphael "Madonna"; and by drama, such as *Death of a Salesman;* [7] and by music, such as Bach's "Toccata and Fugue"; and by mythos, such as the poignant story of "Prometheus Bound"; and by history, such as the Gospel of Christ. It seems to follow that our proper medium may be symbol, art, ritual, history of a certain kind, drama, story, mythos,—and Person.

II

We are thus led to ask about the nature of myth, for it combines both story and drama, and invites music. Myth is not fabrication, as when we say: "That is sheer myth." Myth is a story, dramatic in kind, which adumbrates the origin and destiny of man. It is not "objective history," even if there were such a thing. The story of Adam is myth, not literal description. Adam, *Adamah,* means man, and man means you and me. The original word even hints the ground from which man was made. *The dramatis personnae* of a myth are always you and your neighbor; the time of a myth is always the date on today's newspaper. So there is no need to seek Adam's birth certificate, or the mountain on which Noah's ark came to rest. By the same token, myth is neither logic nor science. The attempt to marshal a warfare between the book of Genesis and modern science is worse than silly, as silly as it would be to propose a battle between sauerkraut and a sunset. They are in different dimensions. Incidentally a true myth will be remembered when our sliderule sciences have all been forgotten, for true myth is addressed to the immemorial

141

questions, "Who am I?" and "Why am I?", which haunt our pilgrimage.

Notice the qualification: a "true" myth. We may not say of myths that "one myth is as good as another," though we have often been guilty of that too quick judgment. When some likeness was found between Babylonian myth and Biblical myth, undiscerning minds leapt to that shallow conclusion: "One myth is as good as another, and therefore the Bible can claim no distinctiveness, let alone finality." A myth is always under at least three tests: One, does it fulfill history's hints and gleams?; two, does it ring in answer to man's hidden life and to his power to view himself?; and, three, is it *aletheia*, the unveiling of the Mystery, with an awestruck sense of the beyond (which we feel when we see a man die), and an *ecstasis* of challenge which obliges us to view our life and to ask "What now shall I do?" If we accept the Christ event as focal, there is a further question: is the myth true to His light? With these comments as a guide we shall now look at certain myths sacred and profane.

As for myths concerning prehistory (the origin of our mortal life), *Pandora's Box* is by and large profane. But since all things come of God it has also a sacred cast. Pandora was so beautiful that her husband, Epimetheus, adored her, thus making an idol of the creature. So at her cajolling he opened the hidden box, thus presuming to know what mortals cannot know. Out flew all the ills, the sicknesses and the crimes, that bedevil mankind. Man's idolatry and presumption bring his sorrow and shame. Thus a myth about the origin of evil: the time is now, and the actors are ourselves. But Epimetheus and Pandora (the man-woman mating) closed the lid of the box quickly enough so that hope did not escape. That is why we still hope. That is the pathos and the glory, for even the word despair, *de spero*, means loss of hope, and thus implies our knowledge of hope. Therefore we must choose between despair and "the courage to be." [8] This story is obviously existential, but it tells us far more about ourselves than biochemistry can ever tell or know.

142

The Tower of Babel is a Biblical myth. Yes, the word Babel shows a Babylonian origin, but the Bible has set on the earlier story a distinctive mark. The earlier story may have been a myth merely about the origin of languages. The Biblical account [9] says that man, in mingled pride and anxiety, resolved to build a tower so high that he could clamber over the rim of heaven to wrest God's throne. In short, man was determined to be his own god: he would completely understand himself by psychology, and completely construe and control his world by rational mind; and, if need be, bomb his way into heaven by his own power. God watched these men with amusement ("He who sits in the heavens laughs"),[10] then destroyed the tower with a finger-flick, and for punishment laid on them "confusion of tongues." Thus the awareness of man's self-destructive pride: "Let us make us a name." Thus the pathetic confession of man's constitutional anxiety: "lest we be scattered abroad over the face of the earth." The story is about us today. Is it true? Have we not tried to be our own god? Have we not dared to claim heaven by our own skill and knowledge? Have our towers not fallen in Hiroshima, London, and Berlin? Do we not now know "confusion of tongues," so that the very word democracy means one thing in Russia and another in the United States, so that Orient and Occident search and search for common ground? The myth is so true that its truth is judgment-agony.

Neither of these myths is literal history or logic or science: they cut to much deeper ground. The second is profounder than the first, for it knows that the question "Who am I?", the question of origin, is in the first instance, "Who are you?" It acknowledges a basic awe. It says with the whole Bible, "It is a fearful thing" (a thing of dread) "to fall into the hands of the living God." [11] "Living," not dead as an ancient idol or a modern abstraction is dead! It views life from above the natural and historical order. It is true to the verdicts of history, to our own deeper awareness, and to the impact of events—and of *the* Event. To despise myth for the sake of some dull factualism is to deny ourselves water from primal springs. So momentous is myth

143

that C. C. Jung has lately proposed, rightly or wrongly, that myth is the archetype of the subconscious mind.[12]

Now we look at certain myths of post-history. They also are legion. They also are sacred and profane, though since God is God and "the earth is the Lord's," [13] the line between the two is not sharp. In Biblical thinking nothing is secular. It can be made secular by man's sin, but in its essential nature it is God's. As instance of a profane myth, made secular by man's pride, consider these words of Mussolini: "We have created our myth. The myth is a faith, it is a passion. It is not necessary that it be a reality. It is a reality by the fact that it is a goal, a hope, a faith, that it is a courage. Our myth is the nation, our myth is the greatness of the nation." [14] The words are astounding both as index of our need of myth, and as evidence of a man's ability to suspect that he is lying and at the same time to cleave to the lie. For of course it is necessary that a true myth "be a reality," for God is Reality and nothing can endure apart from Him. Lenin likewise had his myth, a proletarian world in which all possessiveness shall disappear, and every policeman can be dismissed. These two myths cannot meet either the deeps of our own nature, or the unveilings of history, much less the mind of Christ. What about our American myth of endless and unstayed material progress? All these are myths of post-history, of man's final destiny.

Now ponder a sacred myth of the eschaton, the dénouement of the human pilgrimage: the Biblical story of Armageddon.[15] The Qumran community believed it in literal mind.[16] In desert loneliness, with ablutions and sacramental meals, by indefatigable transcriptions of their Bible, by intensive military maneuvers and disciplines, they prepared for the final battle when the Children of Light would meet and overcome the Children of Night. The end might come next week or the next: even now the Prince of Darkness is marshaling his forces for the demonic onslaught. The Qumran folk did not believe in "evolu-

144

tionary progress"! They did not believe that man by the rationalisms of his mind and the skill of his hand can fashion an earthly paradise! No, man's life is always vulnerable to attacks by the Devil. There are contradictions in human story so tragically dark and real that only the Prince of Light sent by God to lead the faithful into battle can ever resolve them. So a man, any man, must always be on guard, living in eternal vigilance with spirit prepared and purified. The reader must ask himself if the proud hope of modern man or the Qumran realism is truer to our existential nature.

It should be noted that neither myths of prehistory nor myths of post-history attempt any answer to our scientific questions, "when?" and "how?" These questions are important, but in comparison with "who?" and "why?" they are only minor matters. The modern mind is obsessed with the "when" and the "how," but an obsession is only an obsession. The Bible declares that mortal mind cannot know the "when," and can only measurably understand the "how": "It is not for you to know times or seasons which the Father has fixed by his own authority." [17] "Times" in that passage (*kronous*) means the durations of experiences, dynasties, and eras; while "seasons" (*kairous*) means the determinative and crucial events on which history appears to pivot. That is why every "philosophy of history," and much more every "science of history," is confounded. That is why the Bible overrides all science, for science deals only in analytic mind and objective world, while the Bible is centrally concerned with the total life of man under the onsets of the mystery and grace of God in history. All right: myth, historical myth rather than nature myth, can tell us something about our origin and destiny.

III

Now let us turn to history, and centrally to the history of Christ. Here, for the reason repeatedly given in these pages, we may expect to find both fact and interpretation, both event and picture story. The book of Acts, for instance, runs back and forth between the two media—for our deeper understanding. So

145

with the Gospels: the death of Christ on the Cross is historical fact, while the parable of the Last Judgment [18] is by Christ's own word a parable. We are here concerned primarily with the fulfillment of history. What do the Gospels, along with the earlier and later books of the New Testament, tell us about man's destiny? And does the testimony square with our existential self-knowledge, and with all history's revealings? We choose only three words from an immense dictionary of meaning. Yet they are central words to which the other words come for light.

One word is judgment. The *locus classicus* is Christ's story of the Great Assize.[19] This is story, not science or even rigidly logical theology, for story is a better medium of existential truth than either science or theology. Christ does not sit on a throne such as our thrones, and if he did he would be but one more earthly monarch. What does the story tell us? That we live and die under judgment. Every crisis, and every "ordinary event" if we have eyes, reveals the life we have lived. The Greek word *krisis*, from which our word comes, means judgment even more than it means cruciality. According to a modern play [20] an artist dies almost at the moment when art critics recognize that his work is genius. Then? Then the man from whom the artist had rented a garage room claims that the pictures are his: the artist, he says greedily, gave him first right to them. His wife claims that she has been the artist's inspiration: she covets status. The young cook in the house, illiterate but sensitive, with whom perhaps the artist had been in love, claims nothing, but explains pathetically that "snow is not white," because he had shown her that it is "blue." Each of the three stood revealed by human crisis.

Then what of the final crisis called death? The beginning and the end: these are the events from which each of us measures life. Death in particular is delineation. The page on which we write is only so long, and thus our writing becomes an art and craft, an obligation and a verdict. We say as we read the obituary column, "Poor Joe is dead." Who are we to know if Joe is now "poor"? He may be richer far than the living man reading the newspaper. What we mean by "poor" is that Joe is now under crisis–judgment: his earthly record is written, completed, and cannot now be changed. The adjective "poor" is confession of our own guilt and failure. The day is coming when the blinders which we wear shall be taken from us. We need not too rigorously interpret words such as "sheep" and "goats." We know that there is no untinctured good in humankind, and no unrelieved blackness. But we know also that in life and death some people face the light with whatever pain and lapses, while others face the darkness with whatever compunctions. The light is this: "as you did it to one of the least of these my brethren, you did it to me." [21] The Christ event provides the test, for he is the focus of history. We squirm rather than laugh at such a claim. Not our money now, not our status, not our sputnik skill, but what we do for sick folk (then reckoned demon-ridden) and hungry folk and jailbirds, as under the eyes of Christ: this is judgment both now and in the enduring world.

As for words such as "heaven" and "hell," we have no right to fabricate steel-dogma from the open vitalities of a great story. But equally we have no right to evade issues of life and death. The myth of the Lake of Unending Fire finds small sanction in the Bible. It is there on occasion, but only in apocalyptic lurid imagery, and apocalyptic invades rather than informs the New Testament. Jesus used the word "Gehenna." [22] That may have been the Jerusalem city dump, where rubbish was burned, that health (in society as in man?) might be conserved. "Everlasting damnation" [23] is a poor translation, for the word for "everlasting" refers to the ages into which the New Testament believes history is divided by the advent of Christ, and the word "damnation" could much better be rendered condemnation. "Everlasting" is still a timebound word, for no man can reach beyond time by piecing together bits of time without cessation. "These shall go into the darkness of the old era: these into the light of the new world in Christ." [24] But such a translation gives us no

147

"flattering unction." [25] A half century which has passed through two world wars and come on Buchenwald [26] may hardly assume that there is no hell. The proposal insults both our intelligence and our sense of justice—and the agony of our failure. But if in Christ we have the self-disclosure of God, hell cannot be vindictive: it must be remedial. If it be final, is not God defeated? We do not know. We cannot trace the lines of that other dimension of life, much less print on it either our bland universalisms or our cruel dogmatisms. What we are told is that our idolatries, with ourselves at the center of the world, cannot issue in Light; and that to live toward Christ, seeking his pardon both in our bad and in our imagined good, cannot issue in darkness.

The next word is resurrection. The word is not immortality. Immortality is a word of Greek context, with Gnostic implications. It occurs two or three times in the New Testament, but not with its original Gnostic meanings. To the Greeks, man was conceived as a "soul" in a body. The "soul" is like a drop of pure water away from the Oversoul, the Eternal Ocean; the body is the prison of the "soul," and therefore the work of some evil demi-urge. All "souls" are alike. Bodies are different (that is why we are able to recognize one another), but bodies are misfortune. The prison handicap of the body can be blunted in its sharp intrusion by contemplation while we live, but true deliverance must wait on death, for then each man will "have shuffled off this mortal coil," [27] and the pure drop of water will be gathered back into the eternal ocean—and there be lost. This Greek view has large holdings in the modern mind: that is why we quote the Shakespeare line. It has a foothold even in the Church, as when preachers discuss "the immortality of the soul," or when they quote with approval such a falsity as "the soul of salvation is the salvation of the soul." The New Testament has no such word as "soul": "What shall a man give in exchange for his soul?" should be translated, "What shall a man give in exchange for his self?" [28]

The Biblical view of man is that he is a psychosomatic unity.

148

There are "spots" of Gnosticism in the New Testament, but they are not characteristic. To faith in Christ the body also is momentous: a person is a person only as he is body-spirit. Thus salvation involves the whole man. It involves his body as well as his spirit, and body means also all the corporate structures in which his earthly life is lived. The body is not prison. It limits our life, but at the same time gives it instrument—brush, palette, color, and canvas for the artist's work. If the body were only prison, our homes (and our children!) would be devil's scheming, and our daily toil (including medicine and psychiatry) would be only a tinkering with evil stuff. These items have sharp concern with the fulfillment of history. Man's life on this planet is, by Biblical thought, not corrupt. It is in paradox, it defeats all our horizontal ideas of "progress," it cries aloud for redemption because it is fragmentary and wicked and tragic; but it is not bad in its constitution. No, it is a candidate for "resurrection." Body and psyche are alike precious in God's sight. Waving trees and the whole world of nature, along with human faces and the whole pilgrimage of man are cherished in an unseen World, and there shall find fulfillment. Thus Paul Tillich: "The symbol of resurrection points to the truth that the totality of personal life, including the human body, belongs to the ultimate meaning of existence." [29]

So the New Testament gives warrant to the Apostles' Creed: "I believe in . . . the resurrection of the body." Resurrection does not mean either the resuscitation or revival of the flesh, but the lifting of personhood (and of history) in both its terms, *soma-psyche*, into a new and undreamed of dimension of life. Resurrection, because it concerns post-history, can be described only in metaphor and symbol. Resurrection is not thereby invalidated: metaphor and symbol are better carriers of real truth than science and logic. Both Jesus and Paul (following Jesus) described resurrection under the metaphor of a seed. Jesus said, "Unless a grain of wheat falls into the earth and dies, it remains alone; but if it dies, it bears much fruit." [30] Paul, echoing his Lord, said, "What you sow does not come to life unless it

149

dies." [31] The seed dies: the New Testament nowhere evades the stark word "death"; but from death comes flower or tree to harvest. None could guess such beauty and fruitfulness by looking at the seed. Yet the seed is not worthless, for without it there could be no miracle of harvest. Thus our mortal life. It is as unpromising in appearance as a seed—and as filled with promise. It is not itself (in human history) fulfillment, for it is destined to die. Yet it is not under condemnation, for from it comes a new and undreamed of "heaven." Little more is told us: seed in the bin cannot understand waving grain fields. Thornton Wilder has caught this hope when in the play *Our Town* he has the dead speaking to one another from their graves, and saying of those who come to weep in the graveyard that they are like people "shut up in little boxes"! [32] The wonder of the new life is as incredible as our incredible birth into this world.

So the third word is heaven. How much can we know about this promised fulfillment of history? We ask the question in the light of the resurrection of Christ, a fact so sure to his first followers that they wrote the New Testament without one in memoriam line, and fashioned a Church which is so far from being a funeral-benefit society or a company singing dirges round a grave that its members have as central title, "witnesses" [33] to the resurrection. Surely Rudolf Bultmann is insufficient in his theology at this point.[34] There is little evidence that the disciples came to a doctrine of the Resurrection by feeling under the impact of the tragedy of the Cross that this could not be the end. The Resurrection accounts bristle with difficulties; and in any event we were not there, and therefore may not dogmatize about the original experience. But the Resurrection has all the marks of historicity: the instigation is not from the "feelings" of the disciples, but from Christ Himself in such a way that the disciples, taken in breathless surprise, identified him as risen Lord. That is to say, the Resurrection accounts, though they differ, all reflect the uniqueness, the invasion, the historical contingency which belong to an Event; and which cannot belong to our "feelings" alone or to the formulation of our doctrines. This Richard R. Niebuhr seems to me to have shown. His whole study of "historical reason" blazes a new trail, and he is here a safer guide than Rudolf Bultmann.[35]

Then what may we know of history's fulfillment? A focal passage for our guidance is Christ's conversation with the Sadducees about resurrection. They denied it, accepting nothing except the literal interpretation of "the law of Moses." They plied Jesus with their stock question, which was intended to bring the whole debate into ridicule, about the woman who under levirate law married seven brothers in turn: "In the resurrection, therefore, to which of the seven shall she be wife? For they all had her." A major meaning to be gathered from Christ's reply, a deduction from his reticence, is that resurrection is a dimension of life which our earthbound minds can only dimly glimpse: "For in the resurrection they neither marry nor are given in marriage." [36] This answer is no disparagement of marriage, much less of the love which binds a man and woman in the marriage troth. It does not blacken our hope that such love shall persist. But it does hint a range and depth of life, described only as being "like the angels in heaven," [37] which our minds can as little trace as a blind man could describe Lake Louise or a man born deaf can explain for us "the Ninth Symphony." But are there, beyond this reticence, more specific revealings about history's fulfillment?

This: present history is not thrown into the discard. "Have you not read in the book of Moses"—a shrewd thrust, for the Sadducees built their denials on the book of Moses—"how God said to him, 'I am the God of Abraham, and the God of Isaac, and the God of Jacob'?" [38] The verb is present tense: "I am," not, "I was." Thus the mysterious contemporaneity of all history is explicitly avowed. We say, "The past is past," but what we should say is, "The past is present." An event in its strangely invasive nature enters the vitalities of history, and there energizes. A man as he reads history becomes responsible: "that the blood of all the prophets, shed from the foundation of the world, may

151

be required of this generation." [39] In like manner the blessing and curse of the past rests on every man in every generation. Thus there is a sense in which the past is not unchangeable: under the grace of God a man may overcome its curse; under egocentricity he may spoil its blessing; and for good or ill he may carry or refuse to carry its burden.

By the same token, the past is declared to be seed, with all history, of the harvest of a new dimension of life: God "is not the God of the dead, but of the living." [40] The past is living, and moves towards life, not in what modern man calls "progress," but in the vicissitudes of fateful freedom under the sovereignty of God. The whole passage would seem to promise some form of memory in the hereafter, for personhood involves memory. Amnesia is the sterilizing of personhood. Rip Van Winkle is story,[41] not fact: a sleep during which a man's life remains static while his living world of men moves on would be in very truth a sleep of death. Jesus hinted that hereafter his hearers would recognize the stalwarts of their race, Abraham and Isaac and Jacob, though with new eyes and a new memory.

This also: to deny the resurrection is a kind of blasphemy: "You are wrong, because you know neither the scriptures nor the power of God." [42] The scriptures are history within history, the clue to total history; and, since God is God, His plans do not miscarry. His power is not defeated by our mortal contingency: He made us and the contingency, and cannot be the victim of His own work. To assume it would make all history a lunatic chaos. God was not at His wits' end when He fashioned this little spinning ball. He is not a tinpot monarch ruling only over an evergrowing graveyard. God is God. In this world we hear only five finger exercises: hereafter we shall hear symphonies in an unimagined music. This Kipling understood when he said that artists hereafter shall have "brushes of comets' hair" and "splash at a ten league canvas." [43] This the book of Revelation knew when it tells, in what is surely the finest instance of repetition in all literature, of "harpers harping with their harps." [44]

152

The man who jokes about heaven's harps proclaims himself a dolt. These descriptions are inevitably in the earth dimension, but they are straining within history towards the beyond history. God is God: He is not locked in our mortality, or disfigured by history's dark paradox. Hereafter there is a land of golden streets and pearly gates, with no one trying to steal either the gates or the sidewalk; a land where our discords are resolved in music which is an agony of joy, and where trees bear fruit every month, their very leaves bringing healing to the strife of nations.[45]

There is a further implication in Christ's reticent promise of post-history: each generation has its word from God and for God. Not only is each man precious, though he may seem to be tossed on history's tides: each generation has its own gift and witness. For names such as "Abraham and Isaac and Jacob" are of generations, not solely of men. Here is the Bible rebuke of our too "rugged individualism"; here is the avowal that personal experience is grounded in the social life, yes, and gathers meaning from all history. The phrase "Abraham *and* Isaac *and* Jacob" implies the oneness of our human story, the pledge that all history shall be gathered back into a symphony in which its discords shall be resolved in a vast music. No man can be fully saved until his generation, with its wars and factories and drab cities, is saved; and no generation can see redemption until all generations have been gathered home. This the Epistle to the Hebrews clearly tells us, for it says of the heroes of the faith that "they without us should not be made perfect," [46] as we cannot find fulfillment except as those who follow us shall be redeemed.

We live in a space age. Some astronomers guess that there may be many planets with climatic conditions like those we know, and that these other earths may be temporary dwelling of life like our life. We cannot yet tell. The Bible speaks of range on range of life. Its repeated reference to angels makes clear the Bible faith that God's creative power is only distantly hinted by our world. Shall we not say, therefore, that God is pledged not only to fill our history's tragic gaps, to resolve its paradox,

153

to assuage its griefs and sins, but also to gather our history with other ranges and reaches of life into a grandeur which our present mind can only dimly conceive? Maybe our history is only a dissonant chord in a "New World Symphony." This Alice Meynell has proposed:

> Nor, in our little day,
> May His devices with the heavens be guessed,
> His pilgrimage to thread the Milky Way,
> Or His bestowals there be manifest.
>
> O, be prepared, my soul!
> To read the inconceivable, to scan
> The million forms of God those stars unroll
> When, in our turn, we show to them a Man.[47]

So Christ spoke about resurrection. God sealed His word when He raised Christ from the dead. He thus saves history from its own inversion, and gives meaning to our human story. As for me, unless this be the meaning, I can find no meaning.

IV

"What shall I more say?" [48] This: the pledge of history's fulfillment cannot be turned into our presumption. It is not man's role to live in dream conjecture of the world to come, much less to dogmatize greedily about heaven and cruelly about hell. Perhaps part of the reason why our eyes cannot pierce beyond history is that we should not be distracted from present witness. To moon over heaven is a poor escape. Here and now we live; here and now we are to respond to events and to the Event, as our pilgrimage on earth's horizontal path is cut by vertical light. Any follower of Christ who remembers how his Lord was concerned only for the redemptive will of his Father, and thus for the bringing of abundant life to all men, must be appalled at the egocentricities of the average hymnbook.

> Blessed assurance, Jesus is mine!
> O what a foretaste of glory divine! [49]

154

has its priceless truth, for life's vital center is in the person; but it is not the whole truth, for each man's prime concern in history is first with love for God who finds him through the Event, and then with love for his fellowman. The great hymns break in waves of praise of God, and in devotion to the "Beloved Community." The fulfillment of history can come only from beyond history, but it comes also in and through history as men bear their witness to Him who holds history in the hollow of His Hand.

But there is counter-warning: we are not to live as though history were an end in itself, for its end is beyond itself. Even now we are not locked in this world: we have power to view both our own life and the created order of nature and history. The glib phrase, "one world at a time," should carry no conviction. Henry Thoreau spoke the words in his final sickness.[50] If he meant that even in death he would not be distracted from his witness in history, he was exactly right; if he meant that man's life is in only one dimension (such a meaning was not in character with him), he can claim no truth. We live in two dimensions moment by moment. History is a crux of two worlds at a time: "bright shoots of everlastingness"[51] again and again pierce us from above this mortal pilgrimage. Thus Jesus: "He that loses his life" (in its solely mortal dimension) "will find it"[52] (in its higher dimension). When a child dies, or a million men in war, we ask "Why?"—the age-old question of destiny; and we would be heartless if we did not ask. Biblical faith is irreconcilably eschatological. History, by Biblical faith, is a dialectic between two worlds: "Whosoever therefore shall confess me before men, him will I confess also before my Father which is in heaven."[53] We should not be distracted from a joyous witness in history, but the witness itself is to a world above history.

V

The plea of these chapters is that history finds meaning only in an act of faith. No man can successfully print his pattern on history, for history will always confound him. There may be

155

some wisdom in a comparison between the ancient Sinic civilization and the strange planetary nuclear civilization of our time, but there may be equal absurdity. The origin and destiny of history are hidden. The historian, breathing his little span of years in the midst of our pilgrimage, cannot "explain" his own history, much less the strange junctures and complexities of the human odyssey. To propose a "science of history" is a thing incredible: the cycles of nature do not apply to the fateful vitalities of human freedom, for each event in history is unique, as every person is unique. To posit an "evolution in history" is to borrow again from the world of nature, or from a supposed "technological advance"—which may yet be the instrument of our destruction. Increase in scientific knowledge can grant no symbol for the crucialities of personal life. Notice this: any pattern, if it could apply, would destroy freedom; for we would each then become a tiny curve or an inch-line in the pattern. There is an added and equally momentous "reason" for faith: we are not permitted to be spectator historians. Each of us as whole man must play his part in the life drama.

So wise men do not forget the Abyss. They inquire, as indeed all men must, for a faith by which to live. It is now fashionable to live within a ship called Nature-History without asking about the sky above, the deeps below, and the uncharted ocean. It is easy to examine the ship by means of multiple sciences, and to admire it by what we call "the amenities of our culture," but this is escape—which to comfort itself calls Biblical faith an escape! It is still easier to clutch at things and status until breath ebbs. But ever and again we look through the porthole, and then we ask "Who?" "Whence?" "Whither bound?" To forget the Abyss is to deliver life to meaninglessness. Our atheisms have brought us almost to that empty midnight. We cannot ultimately deny God except by suicide, as Albert Camus realized,[54] and suicide may be to leap into His more piercing light. Yes, history is torn, as our individual history is torn, but the very rent implies another world. To disavow the Mystery is to be capsuled in very fact. By some saving grace we do not reach that point of

156

no return. Even a pluralistic university continues to speak about Truth, Value, and Reality. To confess the Mystery, even if we believe we must be utterly agnostic concerning it, is better than to live in dust.

The Christological decision remains. To say that is not "sectarianism" or "obscurantism": it is the very opposite of any "ism," for it confronts us with the existential choice. The issue concerning Christ is not now a question of "two natures." Nature is static or cyclic, and we in our strange time are involved (and how deeply involved!) with the vital world of history. History newly poses the old question: "Then what shall I do with Jesus who is called Christ?" [55] History is one, past and present ever straining towards some future. From what angle may we rightly view history? In what mood shall we contemplate its grief and joy? What event is focal, so that all events may be construed in its light? One Man has split history into before and after, a fact which does not coerce, but which surely beckons. Who in our human story can lead the tragedy of history into joy beyond tragedy? Where shall we find tidings of that Mystery in Whom all history is held? These are the questions. Are they not but different versions of the question about Christ? Spengler wrote better than he knew when, in that strange book which tries to find in nature the clue to history, he wrote: "We await to-day, the philosopher who will tell us in what language history is written and how it is to be read." [56] Not "philosopher"; there can be no philosophy of history, except as a surmise by which we cannot live: not "philosopher," but Revealer and Savior! Thus W. H. Auden, in profounder understanding:

> The Pilgrim Way has led to the Abyss.
> Was it to meet such grinning evidence
> We left our richly odoured ignorance?
> Was the triumphant answer to be this?
> The Pilgrim Way has led to the Abyss.

157

We who must die demand a miracle.
How could the Eternal do a temporal act,
The Infinite become a finite fact?
Nothing can save us that is possible:
We who must die demand a miracle.[57]

A miracle is not some poor rending of the natural order, but an Event which seizes us as the news of God, the invasion of history from beyond history—by events and by the Event. History is "the time being": we have heard the glad tidings, and travel in expectation, and await the destined Word.

NOTES

CHAPTER I *The Bible and History*

1. David Hume (1711-1776), who almost proposed that the self or "soul" is a chain of "perceptions"—without any chain. See *A Treatise of Human Nature* (New York: Oxford University Press, 1928), Bk. 1, Part IV, Sec. VI, "Of Personal Identity," esp. p. 253 ff.
2. Ps. 107:23.
3. Lord Byron, "The Destruction of Sennacherib," st. i.
4. Amos 2:6.
5. Matt. 22:17-22; Mark 12:14-17; Luke 20:22-26.
6. See *Kerygma and Myth*, ed. Hans Werner Bartsch (Harper Torchbooks, New York: Harper and Row, 1961), Rudolf Bultmann: "New Testament and Mythology" and "Bultmann Replies to His Critics." An interesting discussion of the problem can be found in Burton H. Throckmorton, Jr., *The New Testament and Mythology* (Philadelphia: The Westminster Press, 1959).
7. The Apostles' Creed.
8. *A Study of History*, abridgement of Vols. I-VI by D. C. Somervell (New York: Oxford University Press, 1947), p. 37.
9. See William L. Shirer, *The Rise and Fall of the Third Reich* (Crest Book, Greenwich, Conn.: Fawcett Publications, Inc. 1962), pp. 130-33; and Adolf Hitler, *Mein Kampf*, chapters on "Nation and Race" and "The State."
10. E.g., Deut. 7:7-8.
11. See Gal. 3:8. This is also the essential message of the Book of Jonah.
12. Amos 3:2; 5:20.
13. Isa. 40-56.
14. I Kings 22:13-28.
15. II Tim. 4:10 (K.J.V.).
16. Paul Tillich, *Systematic Theology* (Chicago: University of Chicago Press, 1951), I, 110.
17. Exod. 3:14 (K.J.V.), the name by which God revealed himself to Moses.
18. For a discussion of the names of God see *Interpreter's Dictionary of the Bible* (Nashville: Abingdon Press, 1962), II, 410, esp. 3*b*, "I cause to be."
19. Ps. 24:1.
20. Robert Browning, "By the Fireside," st. xlvi.
21. Luther's phrase *opus alienum*, "strange work," in *Werke*, III, 246; XVIII, 633. See also J. S. Whale, *The Protestant Tradition* (Cambridge: Cambridge University Press, 1955), p. 39, and John Dillenberger, *God Hidden and Revealed* (Philadelphia: Muhlenberg Press, 1953), esp. pp. 21, 51, 58, 105, 111-12, 130.
22. Luther's phrase *opus proper*, God as he is in himself, and *ibid*.
23. Gen. 1:4 ff. (K.J.V.).
24. The name of a song in *Flower Drum Song*, by Rodgers, Hammerstein, and Joseph Fields.
25. John Milton, *Paradise Lost*, Bk. I, line 1.
26. A Scottish doctor, journalist, and author (1812-1904), edited *Leed's Times*, author of *Self-Help* (1859); *Character* (1871); *Thrift* (1875); *Duty* (1880).
27. See Thomas Morton, *Speed the Plough* (Philadelphia: Thomas R. Palmer, 1822); name of a farmer's wife mentioned jealously by Dame Ashfield in the play, but never actually appearing.
28. I Sam. 13:14.
29. II Sam. 11:2 ff.
30. Portrait by Sir Peter Lely: "You shall paint me exactly as I am, with all my warts, humors and blemishes." See Samuel Harden Church, *Oliver Cromwell* (New York: G. P. Putnam's Sons, 1894), pp. 396-97.
31. John Keats, "Ode to a Nightingale," st. vii.
32. Ps. 27:1.
33. Ps. 23:1.
34. Jer. 6:14; 8:11.
35. The Nazi concentration camp. See William L. Shirer, *op. cit.*
36. Rom. 3:10, with many Old Testament antecedents, e.g., Ps. 5:9; Isa. 59:7-8.
37. Tr. Justin O'Brien (New York: Alfred A. Knopf, Inc. 1957).
38. "A Tale in Verse and Voices" (New York: Random House, 1953).
39. *A Study of History* (London: Oxford University Press, 1940), V., 317 ff.
40. See Chap. III of this book.
41. Heb. 11:10.

42. *Rubaiydt of Omar Khaydm,* tr. Edward Fitzgerald (New York: George H. Doran Co.), first version, st. lxxiii.
43. Rev. 21:1.
44. Rev. 11:15.
45. E.g., *Civilization on Trial* (New York: Oxford University Press, 1948), pp. 235-36; and *A Study of History, op. cit.,* IV, 35 ff.; and abridged edition, *op. cit.,* p. 253.
46. See Chap. III of this book.
47. Matt. 7:21; 12:50.
48. From a story by Florence Converse, *"Crux ave spec Unica,"* and quoted by Joseph Fort Newton, *His Cross and Ours* (New York and London: Harper and Brothers, 1941), p. 23.
49. *The Myth of Sisyphus and Other Essays,* tr. Justin O'Brien (Vintage Books, New York: Random House, 1961), esp. essay on "An Absurd Reasoning," and *The Rebel,* tr. Anthony Bower (Vintage Books, New York: Random House, 1961), e.g., chs. iii and v; see also Albert Maquet, *Albert Camus,* tr. Herma Briffault (New York: George Braziller, Inc., 1958), ch. iii.
50. *Op. cit.,* p. 24.
51. (New York: Harcourt, Brace & World, Inc., 1950).
52. See, e.g., *The Courage to Be* (New Haven: Yale University Press, 1952).
53. Isa. 55:11 (K.J.V.).
54. From the title of a poem by W. H. Auden, "For the Time Being," *The Collected Poetry of W. H. Auden* (New York: Random House, 1945).
55. *The Interpretation of History* (New York: Charles Scribner's Sons, 1936), p. 264.
56. Rev. 22:20 (K.J.V.).
57. I Cor. 11:26 (K.J.V.).
58. *The Faith of Reason, the Idea of Progress in the French Enlightenment* (New York: King's Crown Press, 1948).
59. From an article "Explanation and Interpretation in History," in *Philosophy of Science,* Vol. 24, No. 2, April, 1957, p. 142.
60. Rev. 13:8 (K.J.V.).

CHAPTER II *The Focus of History*

1. *The Irony of American History* (New York: Charles Scribner's Sons, 1952), p. 151.
2. Oswald Spengler, *The Decline of the West,* tr. Charles F. Atkinson (New York: Alfred A. Knopf, Inc., 1926), esp. Introduction and ch. iii.
3. *The Study of History,* V, 377, 399.
4. Alfred Tennyson, "Vastness," st. ii.
5. *Book of Common Order of the Church of Scotland* (London: Oxford University Press, 1957), p. 176.
6. *Logic, The Theory of Inquiry* (New York: Holt, Rinehart & Winston, Inc., 1938), p. 44.
7. (1833-1911), almost none of his works are translated into English. *Theories of History,* ed. Patrick Gardiner (Glencoe, Ill.: The Free Press, 1959), p. 213, includes an essay entitled "The Understanding of Other Persons and Their Life-Expressions."
8. *The Idea of History* (A Galaxy Book, New York: Oxford Press, 1959).
9. *History, Its Theory and Practice,* tr. Douglas Ainslie (New York: Harcourt, Brace and Co., 1921), Part 1, ch. i, pp. 11 ff.
10. *Op. cit.,* esp. ch. iii.
11. *Ideology and Utopia* (New York: Harcourt, Brace & World, Inc., 1940), pp. 244, 268.
12. "In Memoriam," st. cxxvii.
13. "The Prelude," Bk, XI, "France," 1. 107.
14. "The Widow in the Bye Street," Bk. VI, st. xxvii.
15. In a speech in New York, Nov. 17, 1935, as cited in H. L. Mencken, *A New Dictionary of Quotations* (New York: Alfred A. Knopf, 1942), p. 327.
16. *Cultural Anthropology* (New York: Alfred A. Knopf, 1955), esp. chs. 16, 24, and 25.
17. Phil. 2:5 (K.J.V.).
18. (New York: Alfred A. Knopf, 1962), p. 29.
19. Jacob Burckhardt, *Judgments on History and Historians,* tr. Harry Zohn, with Introduction by H. R. Trevor-Roper (Boston: Beacon Press, 1958), p. xix.
20. Heb. 9:27.
21. An article, "Meaning in History," in *Theories of History,* p. 300.
22. *History, Its Theory and Practice, op. cit.,* p. 12.
23. *The Idea of History, op. cit.,* p. 219.
24. *Civilization on Trial,* p. 27.
25. *Civilization and History* (New York: Charles Scribner's Sons, 1950), pp. 38, 39, 41.
26. *Op. cit.,* pp. 104-13.

27. William Wordsworth, "Intimations of Immortality," 1. 147.
28. Robert Browning, "A Grammarian's Funeral," 1. 97.
29. Shirer, *op. cit.*
30. John 19:22.
31. *The Interpretation of History*, p. 98.
32. William Shakespeare, *Hamlet*, Act III, scene 1.
33. The Apostles' Creed.
34. Gal. 4:4 (K.J.V.).
35. Mark 6:5-6; Matt. 13:58 (K.J.V.).
36. Matt. 24:36; Mark 13:32.
37. Title of a book by Miguel de Unamuno, tr. J. E. Crawford Flitch (New York: The Macmillan Co., 1931).
38. Luke 18:19.
39. A convenient summary of these inquiries (they have their place) may be found in *Theories of History*, in the whole of Part II.
40. Essay on "The Kingdom of God and History" in an Oxford Conference book of the same title (Chicago and New York: Willett, Clark and Co., 1938), Part III, p. 128.
41. *The Idea of History*, pp. 303, 305, 317.
42. *History, Its Theory and Practice*, pp. 134-35.
43. John 1:3.
44. Title of a book by W. H. Auden (New York: Random House, 1947).
45. Jer. 37:17.
46. Attributed to Pythagorus, see *The Works of Francis Bacon* (London: Longmans and Company, 1889), V, 8.
47. Sonnet "On His Blindness."
48. See Note 40.
49. Matt. 22:42.

CHAPTER III *History and Progress*

1. Zech. 9:13.
2. Martin Heidegger, *Being and Time*, tr. John Macquarrie and Edward Robinson (New York: Harper & Row, Publishers, 1962); see Section V.
3. *The Complete Essays and Other Writings*, ed. Brooks Atkinson (Modern Library, New York: Random House, Inc., 1940), p. 67. Address delivered at Harvard Divinity School, July 15, 1838.
4. *Ibid.*, First Series, p. 145.
5. Quoted by Louis Mumford, *The Condition of Man* (New York: Harcourt, Brace & World, Inc., 1944), pp. 305-6.
6. Marquis de Condorcet, *Outlines of an Historical View of the Progress of the Human Mind* (Philadelphia: Lang and Ustick, 1796), Introduction, p. 11. Author has modernized the spelling.
7. Designed by Sir Joseph Paxton in 1851; enlarged and re-erected 1854 in Sydenham; housed war relics, etc., after World War I; destroyed by fire in 1936.
8. *Nausea*, tr. Lloyd Alexander (Norfolk, Conn.: New Directions, 1938). *No Exit*, tr. Stuart Gilbert (New York: Alfred A. Knopf, Inc., 1947).
9. Tr. Stuart Gilbert (New York: Alfred A. Knopf, Inc., 1948).
10. See *The Myth of Sisyphus and Other Essays; The Rebel* esp. Introduction, pp. 5-6; Albert Maquet, *op. cit.*, esp. discussion of "Le Mythe de Sisyphe, L'Etranger and L'Homme Revolte." See also Thomas Hanna, *The Thought and Art of Albert Camus* (Chicago: Henry Regnery Co., 1958), esp. chs. ii, iii and iv.
11. *Op. cit.*
12. Norman Cousins (New York: The Viking Press, Inc., 1945).
13. *Meaning in History* (Chicago: University of Chicago Press, 1949), p. 191.
14. Jean-Paul Sartre, *Being and Nothingness*, tr. Hazel E. Barnes (New York: Philosophical Library, 1956), esp. Part I, ch. i, "The Problem of Nothingness."
15. *What Is History?* See general argument of ch. v, "History as Progress."
16. *Op. cit.*
17. *Faith and History* (New York: Charles Scribner's Sons, 1949), p. 163. The H. G. Wells quote, in the original, is in *Mind at the End of Its Tether and The Happy Turning, A Dream of Life* (New York: Didier, 1946), p. 4.
18. The sell-out to a "science of history" persists. Thus Frederick J. Teggert proposes that we must "attempt to do for human history what biologists are engaged in doing for the history of the forms of life." See *Theory and Processes of History* (Berkeley and Los Angeles: University of California Press, 1960), Introduction to "The Processes of History," p. 223.

19. *Op. cit.*, pp. 83, 170.
20. Shirer, *op. cit.*
21. Lloyd Morgan, *Life, Mind, and Spirit*, Gifford Lectures, 1923, under general title of "Emergent Evolution" (New York: Henry Holt, 1926).
22. John 1:6.
23. See my *Biblical Thought and the Secular University* (Baton Rouge: Louisiana State University Press, 1960), ch. ii.
24. William Shakespeare, *Merchant of Venice*, Act III, scene 2, 1. 78.
25. *Op. cit.*, e.g., pp. 185, 190-94.
26. *The Study of History.*
27. See his essay on "Historical Explanation" in *Mind*, a quarterly review of psychology and philosophy, Vol. LII, July, 1943, p. 227, where he includes a quotation from C. G. Hempel in "The Function of General Laws of History."
28. *Study of History.* See Vol. IV, pp. 28, 33, 35-38; Vol. VI, pp. 173, 324-25.
29. *Lectures on the Philosophy of History*, tr. J. Sibree (London: George Bell and Sons, 1890), Introduction, p. 18.
30. *The Presence of Eternity* (New York: Harper & Row, Publishers, 1957), p. 150.
31. Dachau: See William L. Shirer, *op. cit. Rover Boys:* written by Arthur M. Winfield (New York: Grosset and Dunlap).
32. *The Satires of Decimus Junius Juvenalis*, tr. William Gifford (London: W. Bulmer and Co., 1806), Satire VII, v. 71.
33. *The Myth of Sisyphus and other Essays; op. cit.*
34. Arthur Hugh Clough, *Poems*, "Say not, the Struggle naught availeth" (Boston: Ticknor and Fields, 1862), p. 280.
35. *Op. cit.*, pp. 103-4.
36. I Kings 19:4 (K.J.V.).
37. *Op. cit.*, implicit in his whole discussion of "Dasein." See also John Macquarrie, *An Existentialist Theology* (New York: The Macmillan Company, 1955), pp. 32-33, 42.
38. W. H. Auden, *Poems* (New York: Random House, 1934), The Dedication to Christopher Isherwood.
39. *The Idea of History*, p. 247. H. Richard Niebuhr, *Resurrection and Historical Reason* (New York: Charles Scribner's Sons, 1957) is also highly significant in this regard.
40. *Op. cit.*, p. 96.
41. J. D. Salinger (Boston: Little, Brown & Co., 1951), ch. xxii, p. 224.
42. *The Fathers* (New York: G. P. Putnam's Sons, 1938), Part II, "The Crisis," pp. 185-86.
43. Henry Vaughn (1622-1695), "The Retreat." See *Lyra Mystica*, ed. C. C. Albertson (New York: The Macmillan Co., 1932), pp. 87-88.
44. William Wordsworth, "Elegiac Stanzas (Peele Castle)," l. 15.
45. (a) The American astronaut, John Glenn, see the *National Geographic Magazine*, June, 1962.
    (b) The Russian astronauts, Gherman S. Titov, see *Newsweek*, Aug. 14, 1961, and Pavel R. Popovich, see *Newsweek*, Aug. 27, 1962.
46. The answer to the question, "What are the parts of a Sacrament?" See *The Book of Common Prayer* (New York: Oxford University Press), p. 292, or The Westminster Confession of Faith and Catechisms (1729), The Larger Catechism, Question 163.
47. See *Memorials of Edward Burne-Jones*, by GB-J (New York: The Macmillan Company, 1906), Vol. II, ch. xxv, p. 257.
48. In *Sermons Preached in a University Church* (Nashville: Abingdon Press, 1959), p. 205.
49. Ps. 106:48.
50. Eph. 4:13.
51. *The Interpretation of History*, p. 138.
52. A prayer by James Martineau, *Home Prayers* (London: Longmans Green and Co., Ltd., 1892) and included in Morgan Noyes, *Prayers for Services* (New York: Charles Scribner's Sons, 1937), p. 38.

CHAPTER IV *History as Paradox*

1. Auguste Comte, *Positive Philosophy*, tr. Harriet Martineau (New York: D. Appleton Co., 1854), Vol. II, ch. xii, pp. 450-52. See also J. B. Bury, *The Idea of Progress* (New York: The Macmillan Co., 1920), p. 300.
2. *History*, Bk. 1, ch. xxii, sec. 4 (about 410 B.C.) See also *Plutarch's Lives*, rev. A. H. Clough (Boston: Little, Brown & Co., 1910), III, 382, "Life of Sertorius," where Plutarch speaks of coincidences and "similarity of results," and adds "the same [events] must often recur, and in the same sequence."

3. Alfred Tennyson, "Locksley Hall Sixty Years After," st. 64.
4. Matt. 2:23 (K.J.V.), and see also *The Interpreter's Bible* (Nashville: Abingdon Press, 1951), VII, 261-62.
5. Isa. 53:3.
6. Alfred Tennyson, "Idylls of the King," "The Passing of Arthur," 1. 409.
7. E.g., *A Study of History*, V, 477; VI, 284-87, 305, 312 ff.
8. Esp. pp. 9, 213-14, 302 ff., 324.
9. *The Complete Works of Friedrich Nietzsche*, ed. Oscar Levy, tr. Anthony M. Ludovici (Edinburgh: T. N. Foulis, 1909), I, 50, 183. For an interesting discussion of Nietzsche see an essay by John E. Smith, "Nietzsche: The Conquest of the Tragic Through Art," in *The Tragic Vision and the Christian Faith*, ed. Nathan A. Scott (New York: Association Press, 1957).
10. Quoted by J. S. Whale, *Victor and Victus* (Cambridge University Press. 1960), p. 20, as follows: "Either God cannot abolish evil or he will not. If he will not is he good? If he cannot is he God?" My summary closely approximates the refrain in Archibald MacLeish, *J. B.* (Boston: Houghton Mifflin Company, 1949). See also Augustine *De Origine*, Bk 1, ch. 1.
11. Matt. 16:3; Luke 12:56.
12. William Shakespeare, *Hamlet*, Act V, scene 2, 1. 10.
13. See pages 55 ff. of this book.
14. Immanuel Kant, *Eternal Peace and Other Essays*, tr. W. Hastie (Boston: The World Peace Foundation, 1914), p. 8, in an essay entitled "The Natural Principle of the Political Order, considered in connection with the Idea of a Universal Cosmopolitan History," (1784).
15. Conceived by Hanna and Barbera and found currently in such newspapers as the *Chicago Daily News*.
16. American writer of popular stories for boys (1834-1899). See H. R. Mayes, *Alger, A Biography Without a Hero* (New York: Macy Masius, 1928).
17. Shirer, *op. cit.*
18. *Civilization on Trial*, pp. 11-12. See also *A Study of History* (abridgement), pp. 62-65.
19. *The Survival of Western Culture* (New York: Harper & Brothers, 1943), p. 208.
20. Robert Burns, "To a Mouse," st. vii.
21. Edwin Arlington Robinson in "John Brown," *Collected Poems* (New York: The Macmillan Co., 1927), p. 487.
22. See pages 49 ff. of this book.
23. See *Theories of History*, esp. pp. 158 ff., sec. 7 and 8; p. 141, note 3; pp. 152-55.
24. Spoken to his son, Horace. See Alex Charles Ewald, *Sir Robert Walpole* (London: Chapman and Hall, 1878), p. 453.
25. Shirer, *op. cit.*
26. "The Nicene Creed."
27. A principle formulated by the Danish physicist, Niels Bohr. See article "On Notions of Causality and Complementarity" in Science, Vol. III, January 20, 1950, especially p. 54. See also William G. Pollard, *Chance and Providence* (New York: Charles Scribner's Sons, 1958), pp. 138, 141.
28. *Op. cit.*, pp. 269 ff., in section on "Two Directions in Epistemology."
29. *A Study of History*.
30. *A History of Europe* (Boston: Houghton Mifflin Company, 1935), Preface, p. xv.
31. Carr, *What Is History?* p. 52; Toynbee, *A Study of History*, V, 414; Frankel, *op. cit.*, see ch. i; note 59. Niebuhr, *The Self and the Dramas of History* (New York: Charles Scribner's Sons, 1955), p. 50.
32. "Can We Know the Patterns of the Past?" over B.B.C., January 4 and March 7, 1948, reported in *Theories of History*, p. 318.
33. *Ibid*.
34. April 10, 1932. Quoted by John Finley in his tribute to "The Admirable Ambassador" in *Jean Jules Jusserand* (New York: Jusserand Memorial Committee, 1937), p. 30.
35. John 1:14 (K.J.V.).
36. Col. 1:17 (my translation). R.S.V. translates this "in him all things hold together."
37. Morton, *op. cit.* (See chap. I, note 27.)
38. Shirer, *op. cit.*
39. Matt. 6:22-23.
40. I Cor. 2:14.
41. "The Nicene Creed."
42. *The Study of History*, VI, 278-321.

43. From John Hunter, *Devotional Services* (London: J. M. Dent and Sons, Ltd., 1924), General Prayers, p. 279. This prayer can also be found in Morgan Phelps Noyes, *Prayers for Services* (New York: Charles Scribner's Sons, 1937), p. 221.
44. Acts 1:7.
45. *Gray's English Poems*, ed. D. C. Tovey (London: Cambridge University Press, 1904), "The Progress of Poesy," 1. 100.
46. See Notes 30, 31.
47. Ps. 42:7.
48. From the carol, "I saw three ships."
49. Heb. 10:9.
50. Ps. 19:9 (K.J.V.). Lincoln spoke these words in his Second Inaugural. See Carl Sandburg, *Abraham Lincoln, The War Years* (New York: Harcourt, Brace & World, Inc., 1939), IV, 94.
51. *Pensées*, tr. W. F. Trotter (E. P. Dutton & Co., Inc., 1940), No. 277.
52. Job 38:4.
53. H. A. L. Fisher, *op. cit.*
54. John 1:14.
55. *Poems*, "East London," sts. 2 and 3.

CHAPTER V *History, Necessity, and Freedom*

1. *History of Civilization in England* (New York: D. Appleton and Co., 1858), Vol. I, ch. i. I have here summarized the argument in pages 4-14. The discussion re suicide is found on pages 19-22.
2. *Op. cit.*
3. *The Role of the Individual in History.*
4. Count Leo Tolstoy, *War and Peace*, tr. Louise and Aylmer Maude (New York: Simon and Schuster, 1942), Bk. XV, Second Epilogue, pp. 1336, 1348, and 1351.
5. Tr. Constance Garnett (New York: Random House, 1939).
6. *A System of Logic* (London: Longmans, Green and Co., 1911), Bk. VI, ch. x, pp. 604 ff.; ch. xi, p. 608.
7. *Op. cit.*, Vol. I, General Introduction, p. 24.
8. *A Study of History*, e.g., IV, 38-39; VI, 312-21; see also VI, 174, 324, the Abridgement, pp. 60 ff., 64, and 556.
9. *Historical Inevitability*, Auguste Comte Memorial Trust Lecture, May 12, 1953 (New York: Oxford University Press, 1955), sec. 3, esp. p. 32.
10. *The Freedom of the Will* (London: Adam and Charles Black, 1958), p. 42 f. The argument is summarized.
11. *Op. cit.*, p. 33.
12. *The Hinge of History* (New York: Charles Scribner's Sons, 1959), p. 89.
13. *Ibid.*, p. 91. Jaspers carries this same idea in *The Origin and Goal of History*, tr. Michael Bullock (New Haven: Yale University Press, 1959), pp. 71, 152-57.
14. *The Rubáiyát*, st. xxvii.
15. *Discourses*, tr. Thomas Wentworth Higginson, 1865, ch. xvi.
16. *Op. cit.*, pp. 10-13.
17. *Ibid.*, p. 7.
18. *Ibid.*, pp. 10-12.
19. Luke 15:19.
20. See J. B. Bury, *A History of Greece* (London: Macmillan and Co., Ltd., 1912), p. 267.
21. Shirer, *op. cit.*
22. See Chap. VII of this book.
23. *Letters and Papers from Prison*, ed. Eberhard Bethge, tr. Reginald H. Fuller (London: SCM Press, 1954).
24. James Weldon Johnson and J. Rosamond Johnson, *The Books of American Negro Spirituals* (New York: The Viking Press, Inc., 1940), Bk. I, p. 51.
25. See Martin Heidegger, *op. cit.* See also John Wild, *The Challenge of Existentialism* (Bloomington: Indiana University Press, 1955), pp. 41, 47, 50, 69, 115; esp. 126-29.
26. John 8:34.
27. E.g., *A Study of History* (abridged), pp. 60 ff., 64, 432-33, 556; *Civilization on Trial*, pp. 11-12.
28. Émile Namer, *Galileo*, tr. Sibyl Harris (New York: Robert McBride and Co., 1931), Bk. I, ch. iii.
29. *Descent into Hell* (New York: Pellegrini and Cudahy, 1949), p. 11.
30. Arthur Miller, *Death of a Salesman* (New York: The Viking Press, Inc., 1949).
31. Published by Consumers' Union of United States, Mount Vernon, New York.
32. Lam. 3:22, 23 (K.J.V.). The R.S.V. has dulled and so misconstrued the first sentence.

33. Johnson and Johnson, *op. cit.* See note 24 above.
34. John 16:12.
35. Quoted *Treasury of Sermon Illustrations,* ed. Charles L. Wallis (New York and Nashville: Abingdon-Cokesbury Press, 1950), p. 57.
36. John 1:14.
37. John 8:31, 32.
38. John 8:36.
39. *Hamlet.*
40. *Ibid.,* 1. 230.
41. See Chap. III, note 17.
42. Title of a song, or "swing" tune by William Harold Hodgson, 1931.
43. See Chap. III, note 31.
44. *The Tragic Sense of Life,* pp. 39-40.
45. Pensées, sec. 3, no. 194.
46. *Ethic,* tr. A. Boyle (Everyman's Library, New York: E. P. Dutton & Co., Inc., 1938), Part IV, Prop. LXVII, p. 187.
47. See Chap. VIII of this book.

CHAPTER VI *History as Revelation*

1. Job 9:10 (K.J.V.).
2. See Charles Dickens, *The Christmas Carol.*
3. Matt. 7:11 (K.J.V.).
4. II Cor. 5:19.
5. *Op. cit.*
6. *The Imitation of Christ,* tr. Edward J. Klein (New York: Harper and Brothers, 1914), Bk. I, ch. xix.
7. *Op. cit.,* p. 315.
8. A line from the song, "Some Enchanted Evening" in Rodgers and Hammerstein, *South Pacific.*
9. Matt. 27:32; Mark 15:21.
10. Job 23:3.
11. Gen. 1.
12. Charles Robert Darwin.
13. Immanuel Kant.
14. *Ibid.*
15. Matt. 1:18 (italics mine).
16. See Chap. II, pp. 41 ff.
17. John Milton, Prologue to *Paradise Lost,* The Argument, 1. 26.
18. Matt. 8:20; Luke 9:58.
19. John 18:36 (K.J.V.).
20. Matt. 19:17; Mark 10:18; Luke 18:19.
21. Mark 10:17; Luke 18:18 (K.J.V.).
22. Luke 23:46.
23. E.g., Matt. 4:17; Mark 1:15.
24. Luke 2:14; the oft-quoted Douai Edition.
25. Choruses from "The Rock," *Collected Poems,* 1909-1935 (New York: Harcourt, Brace & Co., 1930), sec. 7, pp. 199-200.
26. Ps. 119:105.
27. "For the Time Being," *The Collected Poetry of W. H. Auden* (New York: Random House), p. 451.
28. John 1:14.
29. From the hymn, "All people that on earth do dwell."
30. Matt. 6:24; Luke 16:13.
31. Choruses from T. S. Eliot's "The Rock," p. 192.
32. William Shakespeare, *Hamlet,* Act V, scene 1, 1. 36.
33. *The Basic Writings of Sigmund Freud,* tr. Dr. A. A. Brill (The Modern Library, New York: Random House, 1938), pp. 859-61 and pp. 11-12 (id and ego, etc.); also *The Ego and the Id,* tr. Joan Riviere (London: Hogarth Press, 1950).
34. Exod. 3:7 ff.
35. John 14:24.
36. *Op. cit.,* pp. 162 ff.
37. Martin Luther. See Roland Bainton, *Here I Stand: A Life of Martin Luther* (Nashville: Abingdon Press, 1950), p. 185.
38. Cited from reading memory. Source not discovered.
39. E.g., Mark 1:15.
40. John 2:4.

41. John 12:23.
42. *On Heroes, Hero-Worship and the Heroic in History,* Lecture 1, sec. 1. See also Hegel, *Lectures in the Philosophy of History,* tr. Sibree (London: George Bell and Sons, 1890), Introduction, pp. 30-34.
43. Phil. 3:10 (K.J.V.).
44. Rom. 6:3.
45. John 11:50.
46. *Op. cit.*
47. William Shakespeare, *The Merchant of Venice,* Act IV, scene 1.
48. "God's World," *Poems* (London: Martin Secker, 1923), p. 22.
49. Johnson and Johnson, *op. cit.,* Bk. 2, p. 34.
50. Pss. 106:2; 145:4, 6, 12; 150:2.
51. Essay on "The Kingdom of God in History," in book of same title, *op. cit.,* pp. 216-217.
52. *The Study of History* (see Chap. III, note 28), and *Civilization on Trial,* pp. 234-36.
53. Matt. 25:40.
54. Luke 18:8, tr. mine: the article is definite in the Greek text.
55. Rev. 22:20 (K.J.V.).
56. *The City of God,* Temple Classics Edition, ed. F. N. Bussell, Bk. V. ch. xvii (in complete edition), Bk. V, ch. viii (in abridged edition).
57. *Op. cit.,* p. 206.
58. John 1:14.
59. Heb. 10:20 (K.J.V.).
60. I John 5:19 (K.J.V.).
61. I John 5:20-21.

CHAPTER VII *History and Tragedy*

1. In *Electra,* the Sophocles drama. See H. D. F. Kitto, *Greek Tragedy:* A Literary Study (Anchor Books, New York: Doubleday and Company, 1954), pp. 135 ff. and his comparison with Euripides and Aeschylus who used the same theme.
2. Play by Eugene O'Neill; see *Nine Plays* (New York: Random House, Modern Library, 1932).
3. Characters in Charles Dickens' *A Tale of Two Cities.*
4. Rudyard Kipling, *Verse* (New York: Doubleday, Doran and Co., Inc., 1940), "Recessional," st. 3.
5. *Oedipus Rex and Oedipus Coloneus,* Sophocles drama. See note 1.
6. Luke 22:42.
7. Robert Browning, "Cleon," sec. 9.
8. See Evelyn Underhill, *Mysticism* (London: Methuen and Co., Ltd., 1912), ch. ix, "The Dark Night of the Soul."
9. John Gottfried Herder, *Outlines of a Philosophy of the History of Man,* tr. John G. Churchill (London: Luke Hanfard, 1803), Vol. II, Bk. XV, pp. 267-68. The spelling has been modernized.
10. See Aylmer Maude, *The Life of Tolstoy* (New York: Dodd, Mead and Co., 1916), Vol. II, "Later Years," pp. 256-59.
11. Luke 23:28.
12. *Op. cit.*
13. Ernest Jones, *The Life and Work of Sigmund Freud* (New York: Basic Books, Inc., 1957), Vol. III, pp. 278-80.
14. Pensées, sec. 6, no. 347.
15. Lane Cooper, *Aristotle on the Art of Poetry* (New York: Harcourt, Brace & Co., 1913), p. 17.
16. *Op. cit.,* see Chap. III, note 10.
17. Charles Kingsley, "The Three Fishers," st. 3.
18. This statement is an inference from his argument in *Birth of Tragedy,* especially pp. 182-83.
19. See Chap. II of this book.
20. *Op. cit.,* Vol. II, ch. iii, p. 87 f., and ch. xv.
21. See Chap. I, note 59.
22. *Op. cit.*
23. Luke 10:31, 32.
24. *Op. cit.*
25. Quoted from reading memory.
26. See *The Interpreter's Dictionary of the Bible,* IV, 317 ff.
27. John Masefield, "The Everlasting Mercy."
28. Rudyard Kipling, "The Prayer of Miriam Cohen," st. 3.

29. Walter Lowrie, *A Short Life of Kierkegaard* (Princeton: Princeton University Press, 1942), p. 255.
30. *Essays, Philosophical and Theological* (London: SCM Press, Ltd., 1955), in his essay "Prophecy and Fulfilment," ch. x, sec. 1.
31. John 1:47.
32. See Lewis Browne, *Blesséd Spinoza* (New York: The Macmillan Co., 1932), p. 246, actually quoting Friedrich Leopold von Hardenberg (Novalis), 1772-1801, *Fragments*, "Man inebriated with God."
33. *Essays*, especially sec. 4.
34. Mark 1:15.
35. Matt. 26:12; Mark 14:8.
36. I Cor. 11:25.
37. John 18:36.
38. John 10:11.
39. Isa. 53:3; as in Handel, *Messiah*.
40. *Essays*, especially secs. 2 and 3.
41. Alfred Tennyson, "The Princess," Part III, st. 22.
42. *The Christian Answer to the Problem of Evil* (London: SCM Press, Ltd., 1947), pp. 46-47.
43. I Pet. 2:24 (K.J.V.).
44. *The Birth of Tragedy*, p. 35.
45. Fyodor Dostoevsky, *The Brothers Karamazov*, tr. Constance Garnett (New York: The Macmillan Co., 1912), Bk. V, ch. iv, "The Rebellion."
46. John 1:14.
47. Isa. 53:4.
48. See John 21.
49. John 20:19-26.
50. John 20:24-28.
51. John 20:29.
52. *Kerygma and Myth*, p. 42; *Theology of the New Testament* (New York: Charles Scribner's Sons, 1951), tr. Kendrick Grobel, I, 37, 292-313, and esp. 295, 299.
53. Luke 24:15.
54. John 16:8.
55. Johnson and Johnson, Bk. II, p. 136.
56. Matt. 17:5; Mark 9:7 (K.J.V.).
57. Professor of Systematic Theology, Garrett Theological Seminary, Evanston, Illinois.
58. Professor of History of Christianity at the same seminary.
59. Rom. 6:3, 4.
60. Phil. 3:10.

CHAPTER VIII *The Fulfillment of History*

1. Gen. 11:4 (K.J.V.).
2. Robert Browning, "A Grammarian's Funeral."
3. Rev. 5:3 (K.J.V.).
4. Alfred Tennyson, "Crossing the Bar," st. 2.
5. William Wordsworth, "Intimations of Immortality from Recollections of Early Childhood," st. 5.
6. Titov, *New York Times*, May 7, 1962. See C. L. Sulzberger's report of his interview with Premier Khrushchev, *The New York Times*, Sept. 9, 1961.
7. Arthur Miller.
8. Title of a book by Paul Tillich (New Haven: Yale University Press, 1952).
9. Gen. 11:1-9.
10. Ps. 2:4.
11. Heb. 10:31.
12. *The Collected Works of C. G. Jung*, tr. R.F.C. Hull (New York: Pantheon Books, Inc., 1959), Vol. IX, Part 1, esp. p. 5. See also David Cox, *Jung and St. Paul* (New York: Association Press, 1959), pp. 121-29.
13. Ps. 24:1.
14. From a speech in Naples, 1922, quoted John A. T. Robinson, *In the End, God* (London: James Clarke & Co., Ltd., 1950), p. 23; and quoted also by Canon C. Smyth in "Christianity and the Secular Myths," *Theology*, October, 1949.
15. See Rev. 16:16.
16. See, e.g., Millar Burrows, *The Dead Sea Scrolls* (New York: The Viking Press, Inc., 1955), Part 4 and Part 6D.
17. Acts 1:7.
18. Matt. 25:31-46.

19. *Ibid.*
20. Sidney Coe Howard, *The Late Christopher Bean;* see John Gassner, *Twenty Best European Plays on the American Stage* (New York: Crown Publishers, Inc., 1957).
21. Matt. 25:40, 45.
22. For "Gehenna," tr. "hell"; see such passages as Matt. 5:22, 29, 30; 10:28; etc. And consult *The Interpreter's Bible,* VIII, 222.
23. For "damnation," see such passages as Matt. 23:14; Mark 12:40; Luke 20:47.
24. My "free" translation.
25. William Shakespeare, *Hamlet,* Act III, sc. 4, 1. 144.
26. *Op cit.*
27. William Shakespeare, *Hamlet,* Act III, sc. 1, 1. 67.
28. Matt. 16:26; Mark 8:37; Luke 9:25 (K.J.V.). The R.S.V. rightly has "forfeits his life."
29. *The Kingdom of God and History,* p. 121.
30. John 12:24.
31. I Cor. 15:36.
32. *Our Town* (New York: Coward-McCann, Inc., 1938), Act III, p. 111.
33. Acts 1:8; 2:32; 3:15; etc.
34. See *Kerygma and Myth,* pp. 38 ff.
35. *Resurrection and Historical Reason* (New York: Charles Scribner's Sons, 1957), especially ch. vi.
36. Matt. 22:23-33; Mark 12:18-27; Luke 20:27-40.
37. Matt. 22:30; Mark 12:25; Luke 20:36.
38. Matt. 22:32; Mark 12:26; Luke 20:37.
39. Luke 11:50.
40. Matt. 22:30; Mark 12:27; Luke 20:38.
41. See Washington Irving, *The Sketch Book of Geoffrey Crayon* (Everyman's Library), New York: E. P. Dutton and Co., p. 26.
42. Matt. 22:29.
43. "When Earth's Last Picture Is Painted," st. 2.
44. Rev. 14:2 (K.J.V.).
45. Rev. 22:2.
46. Heb. 11:40 (K.J.V.).
47. "Christ in the Universe," sts. 5 and 7, as quoted in Viola Meynell, *Alice Meynell: a Memoir* (New York: Charles Scribner's Sons, 1929), pp. 288-89.
48. Heb. 11:32.
49. From a hymn by Fanny Crosby.
50. *Familiar Letters of Henry David Thoreau* (Boston: Houghton Mifflin and Co., 1895), p. 439, report of a conversation with Parker Pillsbury during Thoreau's last illness.
51. Henry Vaughan, "The Retreat."
52. Matt. 10:39; Luke 17:33; also Matt. 16:25; Mark 8:35; Luke 9:24.
53. Matt. 10:32-33 (K.J.V.); Luke 12:8-9.
54. See *The Myth of Sisyphus and Other Essays.*
55. Matt. 27:22.
56. *The Decline of the West,* ch. i, Introduction, p. 8.
57. "For the Time Being," sec. 3, p. 141.

INDEX OF SCRIPTURE

Genesis 1 104
  1:4 ff. 19
  11:1-9 143
  11:4 138

Exodus 3:7 ff. 109
  3:14 19

Deuteronomy 7:7-8 .. 17

I Samuel 13:14 21

II Samuel 11:2 ff. 21

I Kings 19:4 56
  22:13-28 18

Job 9:10 99
  23:3 104
  38:4 79

Psalms 2:4 143
  5:9 23
  19:9 79
  23:1 22
  24:1 ....19, 144
  27:1 22
  42:7 78
  106:2 113
  106:48 61
  107:23 16
  119:105 107
  145:4, 6, 12 113
  150:2 113

Lamentations 3:22, 23 93

Isaiah 40-56 17
  53:3 ....65, 130
  53:4 132
  55:11 28
  59:7-8 23

Jeremiah 6:14 22
  8:11 22
  37:17 44

Amos 2:6 16
  3:2 17
  5:20 17

Zechariah 9:13 45

Matthew 1:18 105
  2:23 65
  4:17 106
  5:22, 29, 30 147
  6:22-23 76
  6:24 108
  7:11 100
  7:21 26
  8:20 105
  10:28 147
  10:32-33 155
  10:39 155
  12:50 26
  13:58 40
  16:3 68
  16:25 155

Matthew—cont'd
  16:26 148
  17:5 135
  19:17 105
  22:17-22 16
  22:23-33 151
  22:29 152
  22:30 ....151, 152
  22:32 151
  22:42 44
  23:14 147
  24:36 40
  25:31-46 146
  25:40 114
  25:40, 45 147
  26:12 130
  27:22 157
  27:32 103

Mark 1:15 ...106, 110, 130
  6:5-6 40
  8:35 155
  8:37 148
  9:7 135
  10:17 105
  10:18 105
  12:14-17 16
  12:18-27 151
  12:25 151
  12:26 151
  12:27 152
  12:40 147
  13:32 40
  14:8 130
  15:21 103

Luke 2:14 106
  9:24 155
  9:25 148
  9:58 105
  10:31, 32 126
  11:50 151-52
  12:8-9 155
  12:56 68
  15:19 89
  16:13 108
  17:33 155
  18:8 114-115
  18:18 105
  18:19 ....42, 105
  20:22-26 16
  20:27-40 151
  20:36 151
  20:37 151
  20:38 152
  20:47 147
  22:42 120
  23:28 122
  23:46 105
  24:15 134

John 1:3 44
  1:6 50
  1:14 ....76, 80, 96,
        107, 117, 132

John—cont'd
  1:47 130
  2:4 110
  8:31, 32 96
  8:34 91
  8:36 96
  10:11 130
  11:50 111
  12:23 110
  12:24 149
  14:24 109
  16:8 134
  16:12 95
  18:36 ....105, 130
  19:22 38
  20:19-26 133
  20:24-28 133
  20:29 133
  21 133

Acts 1:7 ....77, 145
  1:8 150
  2:32 150
  3:15 150

Romans 3:10 23
  6:3 111
  6:3, 4 137

I Corinthians 2:14 .. 77
  11:25 130
  11:26 29
  15:36 149-150

II Corinthians 5:19 .. 100

Galatians 3:8 17
  4:4 40

Ephesians 4:13 61

Colossians 1:17 76

Philippians 2:5 35
  3:10 ....111, 137

Hebrews 9:27 35
  10:9 79
  10:20 117
  10:31 143
  11:10 24
  11:32 154
  11:40 153

II Timothy 4:10 18

I Peter 2:24 131

I John 5:19 118
  5:20-21 118

Revelation 5:3 139
  11:15 24
  13:8 29
  14:2 152
  16:16 144
  21:1 24
  22:2 153
  22:20 ....28, 115

INDEX OF PERSONS AND SUBJECTS

Abraham, 24, 109; Isaac and Jacob, 151, 152, 153
Absurd, Camus and the, 26-27, 47, 123
Acceptance, Paul Tillich and, 27
Acropolis, the, 37
Acts, book of, 145
Adam, story of, 141
Advancement of Colored People, National Association for, 33
Age of Anxiety, 44, 47
Alethia, 140, 142
Alger, Horatio, 69
American Dream, 17, 138
Andover Hall Address, 46
Anna Karenina, 84
Anne, 23-24
Antigone, 119, 126
Apostles' Creed: and New Testament, 149; quotations, 17, 40
Archaeology, 20
Aristotle, quotation, 123
Armageddon, Myth of, 22, 144
Arnold, Benedict, 33, 55-56, 90
Arnold, Matthew, quotation, 80-81
Assyria, 16, 20, 70
Astronaut, 60, 140-41
Auden, W. H., 47; quotations 28, 44, 56-57, 107, 157-58
Augustine, 67; quotation, 117

Babel, Tower of, 22, 138, 143
Bacon, Francis, quotation, 44
Batista, 116
Believe it or not, Ripley's 34
Berlin, 30, 143; Wall of, 60
Berlin, Isaiah, 85; quotation, 86
Bethlehem, 78, 106, 113
Bible: actuality and accuracy in, 21; and Creation, 105; and fact of death, 146-47; and heaven, 147, 150-54; and hell, 147-48; and judgment, 146-48; and justice, 111-13; and paradox, 76-81; and politics, 16, 19; and resurrection, 132-35, 148-54; and theology, 18, 19, 146; doctrine of God in, 16, 18-20 (*see also* God); doctrine of man in, 15-16 (*see also* Man); doctrine of time in, 15, 93-94, 153-55; freedom and necessity, 91-99; history's brokenness and redemption, 22-25, 27-29, 39-43, 129-132; is eschatological, 24, 152-55; is faith history, 20-22; is focused history, 20, 25-26, 38-44; is sacred history, 18-20; inconsistencies and interpretation in, 15, 16-17, 20-21, 145-46; myth and, 16, 22, 142-44; pain, suffering, and tragedy, 67, 126-37; progress, the wrong word, 55-61; sees history as Dialogue, and the event of Christ clue and crux of history, *see* History, Jesus Christ; sees man's response in faith, *see* Man
Black Plague, 35
"Blood and Soil," 17, 38, 49, 76
B-Minor Mass of Bach, 134
Bonhoeffer Letters, 90

Books of American Negro Spirituals, 90, 94, 113, 134
Britannica Encyclopaedia, 32
Brokenness of history and our age, 22-25, 26-27, 68-69, 139
Brother to Dragons, 23
Browning, Robert, quotations, 19, 37, 102, 120-21, 138
Buchenwald, 23, 90, 122, 126, 148
Buckle, Henry T., 83, 84, 85, 88, quotations, 83, 84
Bultmann, Rudolf, 151; and freedom, 53-54; and fulfillment, 130; and myth, 16; and New Testament study, 16; and resurrection, 133, 150-51
Burns, Robert, quotation 70
Butterfield, Herbert, 36, quotation, 36
Byron, Lord, quotation, 16

Cadman, S. Parkes, quotation, 34
Caesar, 16
Caiaphas, 111
Calvin, John, 33; Calvinism, 82
Calvary, 19, 25, 26-27, 113, 132-35
Camus, Albert, 23, 26-27, 47, 123, 156
Cape Canaveral, 101
Carlyle, Thomas, quotation, 111
Carr, Dr. E. H., 35, 47, 49, 51, 56, 75; quotations, 35, 58, 75, 78
Carton, Sydney, 119
Catcher in the Rye, 59
Catharsis, 123-24, 137
Chess game, 27
Christ. *See* Jesus Christ
Chronicles, Book of, 21
Church: eschatology of, 61; a revelation of God in history, 113-15; and the Cross, 129; and the resurrection, 132-33; Old Testament and early church, 65; early church knew Jesus as Lord, 27-28; and nature worship, 48
Civilization, 59-60, 124, 140; Sinic, 156; our, 11, 92, 97-98
Cleon, 120
Clough, A. H., quotation, 55
Cocktail Party, The, 27
Collingwood, R. C., 32, 43, 66, quotations, 36, 58, 103
Communism, 20, Russian heresy, 104
Complementarity, principle of, 74
Comte, Auguste, 64, 84, 124
Condorcet, Marquis de, quotation, 46
Conscience, humanistic and Freudian, 109
Consumer's Research Reports, 93
Converse, Florence, quotation, 26
Courage, the word, 47
Creeds, the, 40
Croce, Benedetto, 32, 36, 43
Cromwell, Oliver, quotation, 21
Critique of Pure Reason, 104
Critique of Practical Reason, 104
Cross: end of our world and beginning of God's, 131; groups round, 65; story of village cross, 26; to Gospel of Mark, 27; *see also* Jesus Christ

171

Crosby, Fanny, quotation (hymn) 154
Crystal Palace, 46
Cuba, and State Department, 116; Cuban crisis, 59; revolution, 115-16
Cultures, cyclic, 24-25, 30, 32-33, 64, 114, 135

Dachau, 54, 69, 97, 122
Dawson, Christopher, quotation 114
Death: ambivalent about, 98; and Victorian optimism, 54; fact of, 37, 62, 134, New Testament and, 146-47, 150; terror of, 122-23
Death of a Salesman, 141
Declaration of Independence, 90
Decline of the West, The, 47, 84
Defarges, 120
Demas, 18
Descartes, 58
Determinist view of history, 83-86
Deutero-Isaiah, 17
Devil, the, 75, 77, 82, 91, 101
Dewey, John, 31, quotation, 31
Dialectic: Hegelian, 22, 71, 127; Marxist, 22, 25, 71-73, 127
Dialogue between God and Man, prayer and the, 16, 62, 97; see also History, God, Man
Dilthey, Wilhelm, 92
Dracula, 64

Easter, 19, 132, 133, 134
Economics, 16, 19, 58
Electricity, 32, 59
Electra, 119
Elijah, 56
Eliot, T. S., 27, quotations 106, 108
Emerson, Ralph Waldo, 46, 124
Epictetus, quotation, 87
Eschatalogical: Bible history is, 24; Biblical faith is, 155; Mystery, 61
Estes, Billie Sol, 33
Essenes, 40, 65
Esther, 22
European Common Market, 102
Event, of Christ. See Jesus Christ
Events: history a Dialogue in language of, see History; not simple but revelation, 101-4; dominant events of history, 104-18; are miraculous, 59-60; repetitiveness and newness in, 64-66
Evolution: Darwinian theory of, 49; fancied, 24; history and, 156; human nature and, 49-50
Existentialism, 20, 32, 91; Heidegger's, 16; of Scripture, 25
Evil, 39, 77-78; 122-23

Faith: Christianity is historical, 43-44; confronts paradox, 78-81; history, Bible is, 20-22; history finds meaning in act of, 155-58; is man's response, 43-44, 59-61, 80-81, 104-7, 157-58; verdict about Christ by, 43-44; not easy, 63
Faith and History, 12
Faith of Reason, The, 29
Fall, The, 23, 27

Farrar, Austin, 86, quotation, 86
Faubus, Governor, 33
Faust, 69, 85, 101
Fifth Symphony, 60
Fisher, H. A. L., quotations, 75, 77-78
Flintstones, The, 69
Flewelling, Ralph Tyler, quotation, 70
Florida, 27, 116
Flower Drum Song, quotation 19-20
Forgetfulness in historical order, 85
Frankel, Charles, 29, 75, quotations, 29, 35
Freedom: bland use of word, 53-54; God and, 93-95; history struggle for, 90-91; of Jesus Christ, 95-96; relation between necessity and, 86-90; theories of necessity and, 83-86; unpredictable elements in human, 65-66, 69-71
French Revolution, 33
Freud, 123, 131; and conscience, 109
Fulfillment: Bultmann and, 130; Christ and, 129-37, 145-55; history cannot of itself find, 138-39; man in history and, 139-41; myth and, 141-45

Gadgets, an idolatry, 108
Galileo, 92
Gandhi, 110
Gehenna, 147
Genghis Khan, 52
Genesis, Book of, and science, 141-42
Germany, 32, 66, 74, 94, 119
Geyl, Pieter, quotation, 75
Ginza, 74
God: abyss of Mystery, 18-19, 20, 21, 22, 29, 41-42, 51, 57-58, 61-62, 77-80, 99, 101, 112; acts of, 18-19, 20-21, 25, 27-29, and Christ God's final move, 27-29; alien works of, 19; and freedom and necessity, 91-95; and judgment, 17, 146-48; and justice, 111-13; and pain, suffering and tragedy, 39, 67-68, 127-137; and progress, 59-62; as Creator and Lord of History, 18-19, 39, 77-78, 97-101, 27-29, 131, 139, 152-53; Christ self-disclosure of, 19-20, 27-29, 39, 41-42, 79-81, 100-1, 104-7, 117-18, 157-58; every man believes in, 128-29; dialogue between God and man in the language of events and the Event, see History; man's response to God's onsets, see Man; Kingdom of, 105-6, 116; name of, 18-19, 128; not joker in the pack, 58; proof of, 18, 41-42, 127-30; proper works of, 19; power of, 152-53; purpose in Bible history, 17, 19-20, 24-25; revelations of, in history, 18-19, 78, 80-81, 104-7, 107-16; what is God like?, 16, 18, 44, 128-32, 134-35
Gnosticism, 148-49
Golgotha, 122, 134
"Goodwill," meaning of, 106
Gospels: and man's destiny, 146 ff.; core is history, 16-17; interpretation in, 16-17; the Gospel is history, 40
Grace, 17, 58-59, 60, 135-36
Gray's English Poems, 77
Great Assize, Parable of, 146 ff.

Greek, 40; cyclicism, 23; interpretation of history, 45; meanings, 77, 106, 146; thought concerning the planet, reason and soul, 20, 50, and 148
Green, J. H., 34
Grundy, Mrs., 21, 76
Guilt, man's, 41, 76-77

Hallelujah Chorus, 135
Happen, the word, 101
Harvard, 12
Hawthorne, 124
Hayes, Roland, 134
Heaven and Hell, and the New Testament, 147-48, 150-51
Hebrews, Epistle of the, 153
Hegel, 22, 71, 127, quotation 53
Heidegger, Martin: and history, 45; existentialism of, 16; quotation, 56
Herder, Gottfried, quotation, 121
Herskovits, Melville J., 34
Hiroshima, 97, 131, 143
Historian: classified, 34; culture pattern school, 34; confront brokenness and tragedy of history, 35-36, 124-26; history's redemption, 35-38; confront progress, 47-54; confront paradox, 64-76; Marxist, 32; must love the past, 35, 43; must take a stance, 31-33; must take an inner stance, 33-35; objective, 31-32; scientific, 32-33
History: absurd, 26-27, 123; a Dialogue, 13, 20, 44, 45, 60-61, 79-81, 89, 94-98, 118, 127-37; analogy with nature, 32-33, 36, 48-50; Bible, 16-29, see also Bible; Buddhist, 23; event and, 59-60, 64-66, 101-4, dominant events of, 25-27, 104-18, event of Christ clue to, 25-27, 38-44, 104-7, 157; cyclic cast of, 11, 13, 25, 30, 32-33, 64, 114, 135; evolution and, 49-50, 156; faith and man's response to onsets of God in, see Man; focus of, 25-27, 36-44; fulfillment of 138-41, 145-58; God's self-disclosures in, 104-18; Hindu, 23, 33; Greek interpretation of, 45; idolatry and, 107-11; individual concern in, 103-4, 115-16; is transient, 38; is irrevocable, 38; justice and, 111-13; meaning in, 30-31, 67-68; 155-58; myth and, see Myth; necessity and freedom in, 82-83, 86-91, God and, 91-95; paradoxes of, 63-74; and see Paradox; paradoxical because, 74-79, 135; patternless pattern of, 79-81, 129, 156; progress in, 45-62, see also Progress; progress of the race, 52-53; progress, wrong word and measurement, 55-62; philosophy of, 18, 102, 145-57; portent of the church and, 113-15; redemption of, 27-29, 38-43, 61-62, 76-77, 79-81, 127-37, 145-58; revelation in, see God; science of, 32-33, 48, 82-85, 125-26, 145, 156; sickness of, 22-23, 26-27, 36-37; sociology and, 48, 52, 73; theories of, 83-86, 124-26; three events in 25; tragedy and, 35-38, 50, 119-37; witness of prophets in, 109-11

Hitler, 17, 49, 66, 71, 74, 90, 94, 119; Hitlerism, 38, 71
Hume, David, 15
Hus, John, 109

Idolatry, 37, 41, 42, 107-9, 148
Immortality, wrong word, 148
Indoctrination, 38, 40, 63, 101, 108
Individual, the, and progress of the race, 51-53
Isaac, 152
Israel: and commission, 17; history of, 16-19, 129-30, religion of, 15, old and new, 24, 113
Isaiah, Deutero, 17; Second, 24

Jacksonville, 27
Jacob, 152
Jaspers, Karl, quotations, 86, 97-98
Jeremiah, 109
Jerusalem, 103
Jesus Christ: and death, 42, 97-98, 146-47; and judgment, 146-48; and heaven, 147, 150-51; and hell, 147-48; and pain, suffering and tragedy, 42, 105-7, 129-37; and post-history, 153-54; and progress, 60-62; and resurrection, 148-51; beyondness of, 41-43, 105-131; convicts of guilt, 41; cross of, 25, 26-27, 37, 38-39, 42, 67, 70, 77, 79, 83, 90, 96, 105-7, 125, 134-35, 146; Event of, clue to the Dialogue, 13, 43-44, 95-96, 97-98, 117-18, 129-32, 137 and crux or focus of history, 19, 25, 43-44, 58-59, 60-62, 117-18, 147, 155-58; enter paradox of history, 76, 80-81, 96; faith in, is man's response to the Dialogue, 43-44, 59-61, 63, 78-79, 80-81, 103, 104-7, 157-58; fulfillment of history and, 27, 65, 110, 129-30, 145-55; God's final move, 27-29, 131-32; historical reality of, 38-42, 104-7, 137, 146; Parable of the Great Assize, 146-54; proof of, 38-39; Redemption and, 26-29, 38-44, 80-81, 127-37; Resurrection of, 42, 132-35, 148-54; self-disclosure of God, 27-29, 41-42, 80-81, 100-1, 104-7, 117-18, 157-58; split history (calendar), 26, 33, 38, 43, 57, 157; under necessity, yet history's only free man, 95-96; Virgin Birth and, 42
Jews, 17, 94
Job, 22, 111, 120
John, Gospel of, 32
Judgment, 133, 146-48
Jusserand, Jules, quotation, 75
Justice and history, 111-13; Deuteronomic, 111
Juvenalis, quotation, 54
Jung, C. C., and myth, 144

Kafka, Franz, 22
Kagawa, 110
Kairous, 145
Kant, Immanuel, 69; quotation, 68
Karamazov, Ivan, 132

Keats, John, 44; quotation, 22
Kennedy, President, 26
Khrushchev, Premier, 26, 73
Kierkegaard, Søren, quotation, 128
King James Version, 130
Kings, Book of, 21
Kingsley, Charles, quotation, 123
Kipling, Rudyard, 120, 128, 152
Kronous, 145

Laeuchli, Samuel, 136
Lamentations, Book of, 93
Parable of the Last Judgment, 146-54
Learning, 51; an idolatry, 108
Lenin, 71, 72, and myth, 144
Limitation and passion, 119-21
Lincoln, Abraham, 55, 56, 124; Second Inaugural, 55, 90; quotation, 79
Logic, and axiom, 59, 129, 140; and history's fulfillment, 140-41, 149, Marxist, 71-73.
Logic, The Theory of Inquiry, 31
Loman, Willie, 93
Louis XV, 72-73
Löwith, Karl, 47; quotation, 117
Luther, Martin, 19, 109-10

Madonna, Raphael's, 141
Magna Carta, 90
Man: and the Dialogue, *see* History; Biblical view of, 148-49; candidate for resurrection, 149-53; evolution and nature of, 49-50; eyes and nature paradoxical, 74-77; held in freedom and necessity, 86-95; in history, 18, 20, 45, 61-62, 137-40; psyche-soma, not Greek "soul," 50, 72, 87, 148-49; lives at crux of two lines, 56-62; lives two dimensional life, 52, 56, 74-75, 96; origin and destiny of, 30-31, 41-42, 54-57, 74-75, 77-78, 79-80, 139-41, 143-45; questions progress and asks "Am I getting better?", 45, 61-62; response, in faith, 13, 19, 20-23, 29, 43-44, 58-62, 78-79, 80-81, 103-7, 117-18, 137, 157-58; responsible in history, 69-71, 74
Mannheim, Karl, 33, 74-75; quotation, 33
Maranatha, 28, 29
Martineau, James, quotation, 62
Mark, Gospel of, 27
Marx, Karl, 34, 52, 108
Marxism and history 71-73, 127
Masefield, John, 33-34, 128
Matthew, 130
Meliorist view of history, 84-85
Melville, 124
Mephistopheles, 69
Meynell, Alice, quotation, 154
Micaiah, 18
Michaelson, Carl, 86; quotation, 86
Michelangelo, 61
Mill, John Stuart, 84-85; quotation, 85
Millay, Edna St. Vincent, quotation, 112
Milton, John, 21, 44, 47, 105
Mind, nature of, 18, 50-51, 57-58, 82-83; modern, 63; progress of man's, 92

Mississippi, 87, 98
Modern Man Is Obsolete, 47
Morgan, Lloyd, 49
Moses, 109; Book and law of, 151
Mourning becomes Electra, 119
Mussolini, myth of, 144
Mystery: nature of, 141-45; *see also* God
Myth: and the Bible, 22; and the New Testament, 16; Babylonian, 142, Biblical, 142, Bultmann and, 16, of Armageddon, 22, 144; of post-history, 144-45; of pre-history, 142-44, of Pandora's Box, 142, of Babel, 22, 143

Natural Law, 82, 87
Nature, and human nature, blights and leisons in, 19, 23, 35; history and analogy with, 36, 48-50; human nature and evolution, 49-50
Nausea, 46
Nazarene or Nazorene, 65
Nazism, 90
Necessity and freedom: relation between, 86-90; God and, 91-98; History and, 82-83, 90-91; Jesus under, 95-96; no absolute, 87-88; three theories of history concerning, 83-86; Necessity and passion, 120-21
New Testament: and Acts of God, 19; and faith's continuance, 114-15; and man's destiny, 146 ff.; and myth, 16-17; and word "immortality," 148; and word "soul," 148-49; apocalyptic and, 147; Apostles' Creed and, 149; Bultmann and, 16, 151; Early Church had no, 65; Faith of, 117-18; Gnosticism in, 148-49; Grace N. T. word, 60; insight and courage of, 137; no immemoriam word in, 27, 150; Resurrection and, 132-35, 148-54
New Yorker, The, 72
Nicene Creed, quotation, 74, 77
Niebuhr, Reinhold, 12, 30, 47, 75
Niebuhr, Richard R., 151
Nietzsche, Friedrich, 67, 124, 131-32
Ninth Symphony, 151
Noah's Ark, 141
No Exit, 46
Nothingness, 47

Oedipus, 120
Old Testament, 17, 22; God revealed in His wondrous acts, 18-19; Early Church and, 65; fulfilled in Christ, 130
Olympics, professor at, 44
Optimism: American, 16; Hegelian, 22; Victorian and fallacies of, 46, 48-54
Origin of Species, 104
Orphanage, Pennsylvania, 66
Our Town, quotation, 150

Pain, problem of, 67
Pandora's Box, 142
Paradox: what is?, 64; paradoxes of history: repetitive and unique, 64-66; irrational and purposeful, 66-68; progress and retrogression, 68-69; requirement

Paradox—cont'd
and wantonness, 69-71; Marxist pattern and opposing forces, 71-73; true and false, determined and free, social and individual, 73-74; man himself is paradoxical, 74-76; how resolved, 76, 138; a field for faith, 77-81
Pascal, quotations, 79, 98, 120
Passion and limitation, 119-21, 134
Paul: and history, 137; and resurrection, 149
Pessimism: modern, 16, 26-27, 46-47; fallacies of 54-58
Pharaoh, 17, 19
Pharisees, 40, 65
Philosophy, abstractions of, 57-58, 102-3; and pain, 67; intellectual, 18; limited, 102; study of and Hegelian dialectic, 71; of history, 126, 145, 157; of life, 102; truth and, 102; philosophic universalism, 51-54
Pilate, 16, 17
Pity, 121-22, 123, 124, 137
Plague, The, 47
Plekhanov, Georgi, 64, 72-73, 84, 110
Politics and the politician, 16, 19, 20, 24, 30, 58, 68, 93
Pollyanna, 23, 97
Pompadour, Madame, 72-73
Pompeii, 35, 67, 126
Positivism and positivist, 31; and history, 43
Prayer and the Dialogue, 13, 62, 97
Progress: American, 13, 22, 67-68, 120; and history, 45-62, 68-69, 135; and man's life, 56-62; Bible and, 24-25, 55-56; Chamber of Commerce, 11; involves two questions, 45, 61-62; of the race, 51-52; optimism regarding and its falacies, 46, 48-54; pessimism and its fallacies, 46-47, 54-58; wrong word, 55-58, 61-62; what is right word, 59-61; on what line is it measured?, 56-61
Prometheus Bound, 141
Prophet, revelation through, 109-11
Psychology, 82
Psychiatry and psychiatrist, 27, 30, 91, 123, 149
Pusey, President Nathan M., 12

Qumran community, 40, 95, 144-45

Race, the Progress of, 51-53
Reason, 50-51, 57-58
Redemption. See History, Jesus Christ
Responsible man, 69-71, 74, 151-52
Resurrection, 148-54; of Jesus Christ, 42, 132-35
Revelation, Book of, 152
Revelation: a Bible word, 78; and Bible History, 17; and history, 101-18; and the scientist, 101; meaning of the word, 99-100; God's self-disclosures: through the Total Event of Christ, 100, 104-7, 117-18; through a higher justice, 111-13, doom of all idolatry, 107-9, the church, 113-15, the

Revelation—cont'd
individual life, 115-16, witness of the prophet, 109-11, requires responses, 117-18
Rip Van Winkle, 152
Robinson, Edwin Arlington, 70
Role of the Individual in History, The, 72
Roman Catholic, 114
Rorschach test, 30
Rover Boy fiction, 54, 97
Rubáiyát, The, quotations, 24, 86
Russia, 73, 116, 143; Russian Revolution, 52, 72, 122
Ruth, 22

Sacrament, The: in the Early church, 29; a better word than progress, 60-61
Sadducees, 40, 65, 151
Sainte-Chapelle, 60
Saint Joan, 63, 106
Salvation: where is? 38 ff., 149; Tillich and 38; Toynbee and, 36
San Francisco earthquake, 66
Satre, Jean Paul, 46-47
Science: of History, 32, 48-49, 83-85, 121, 125-26, 145, 156; and history, 66, 82; and nature, 36, 66, 78; and truth, 25, 57-58, 102; assumes purpose, 66; biological, 24-82; Freedom, necessity, and, 93-95; givenness of, 93-94, 101; man an object, 20, 94, 140; measurements of, 57-58; no objective, 31; proof of God and, 41; the Bible and, 24, 40, revelation and, 101-3
Scrooge, 99
Sea of Reeds, 19, 24
Second Inaugural, 55, 90
Self-Reliance, 46
"Shadowy Third," 19, 112
Shakespeare, William, quotations, 39, 51, 68, 96, 108, 112, 148
Shaw, George Bernard, quotation 95
Shirer, William L., 74
Short History of the English People, 34
Simon of Cyrene, 103
Sin and guilt, 37-38, 41, 73, 76-78, 91; original, 82; Russian definition of, 73
Sisyphus, 54-55
Shekinah, 127
Smiles, Samuel, 21
Sociology, 52, 82, 93, 127
Sorokin, 64
Soul, Greek interpretation of, 50, 72, 148
Southern states, 33
South Pacific, quotations, 103
Soviet, Paradise, 138; Republic, 71; Union, 120
Splengler, Oswald, 47, 64, 84, 92; cyclic cultures, 30, 32-33, 37, 114, 135
Spinoza, 98, 130
State Department, 116
"Stigma of finitude," 18
Suffering, 42, 67, 105-7, 129-37
"Suffering Servant," 17, 130

Tate, Alan, quotation, 54-60

Tennyson, Alfred, 33; quotations, 30, 33, 64, 66, 131, 139
Terror, 121, 122-23, 124, 137
The Time Being, 28
The Tragic Sense of Life, 41, 127
Theology, 18, 19, 40, 58, 129-30, 146
Theory, three types of historical: determinist, 83-84; meliorist, 84-85; voluntarist, 85-86; tragedy breaks all, 125-26
Thomas, 133
Three Ships, I saw, quotation, 78
Thoreau, Henry, quotation, 155
Thucydides, 64
Tillich, Paul, and acceptance, 27; quotations, 18, 28, 38, 43, 149
Times, doctrine of, 15, 93-94, 96-98, 152-55; history and, 38, 109-10, 138-39; man lives in "the time being," 28
Tintoretto, 127
Toccata and Fugue, of Bach, 141
Tolstoy, 84; quotation, 84; and from *Life of*, 122
Toynbee, Arnold, 11, 64, 92; analogy from ancient China, 66; believed Jews under an illusion, 17; Cyclic view of history, 11, 13, 25, 85, 100, 114, 135; sees in history dialogue between God and Devil (Faust), 69, 75, 85, 91, 100, 101; history's need of salvation, 36; is determinist, meliorist and voluntarist, 85; metaphor of wagon and wheels, 25, 52, 100, 114; our civilization an open end, 11, 85, 100; power of prophet in history, 110; revelation and, 100-1
Tragedy, meaning of the word, 119; comes out of clash between passion and limitation, 119-21; brings, pity, terror and catharsis, 121-24; the Bible and, in Dialogue, 126-29, 135-37, Piercing Event, 129-32 and Resurrection, 132-35
Trevor-Roper, Professor H. R., 35
Truth, nature of, 25, 57-58, 96, 101-2
Twain, Mark, quotation, 46

U-2, 62, 103
Unamuno, Miguel de, quotations, 41, 98, 127
Unauthentic life, 91
Underhill, Evelyn, quotation 121
United States, 116, 143
Universalism, philosophic, 51-54; and Scripture, 25

Vaughn, Henry, quotation, 60, 155
Vesuvius, 35
Virgin Birth, 42
Voluntarist view of history, 85-86

Walpole, Robert, quotation 73
Walsh, W.H., 35-36
War, 34, 46, 56; the truth about our civilization, 140; civil, 88; racial, 107; two world wars, 54, 64, 87, 89, 148; victors in, 108
Warren, Robert Penn, 23; quotation 27
Watson, Philip S., 135-36
Watson, John B., 88
Wells, H. G., 47; quotations, 47, 97
Whale, John, quotation, 131
What Is History? 35
White, Norton, 52
Whitman, Walt, 46, 124
Wilder, Thornton, quotation, 150
Will, freedom of the, 83, 88-89
Williams, Charles, quotation 93
Wordsworth, William, 33, quotations 33, 37, 60, 140
World: is it getting better? 45-46, 61-62; how measured?, 56-62; the Cross, our world and God's, 131; *see also* Optimism, Pessimism

Xerxes, 89

Zealots, 40, 65
Zion and history, 45

Date Due

FEB 20 '78		
APR		
AP		
PR		
MA		
MAY 1		
OCT		
OCT 2		
NOV 6		
NOV 20		
DEC 3		
DEC 14		
JAN 18		

Demco 293-5